Dialectical Behavior Therapy Skills, 101 Mindfulness Exercises and Other Fun Activities for Children and Adolescents

A Learning Supplement

Kimberly Christensen
Gage Riddoch
Julie Eggers Huber

authorHOUSE®

AuthorHouse™
1663 Liberty Drive, Suite 200
Bloomington, IN 47403
www.authorhouse.com
Phone: 1-800-839-8640

First published by AuthorHouse 2/10/2009

ISBN: 978-1-4343-6825-6 (sc)

Library of Congress Control Number: 2008908807

Printed in the United States of America
Bloomington, Indiana

This book is printed on acid-free paper.

Contents

Acknowledgements

This project has been a wonderful journey for me. It has allowed me to work with two incredible individuals, Julie Eggers Huber and Gage Riddoch, and develop an amazing relationship with both of them. I cannot thank Julie enough for all her support and mentorship she has provided me related to the tremendous value of DBT. In addition, significant thanks go out to Gage for sharing his enormous enthusiasm and dedication to children and adolescents. I also thank my first supervisor, Cathy LaGow, for exposing me to DBT and the valuable concepts it brings to therapy. Great big thanks go out to my mentor from graduate school, Dr. Norman James, for believing in me and supporting me. I also thank the people I have worked with in DBT consultation for making our team so incredible, you all rock!! To my friends and family thank you so much for being patient with me and supporting my endeavors. I couldn't have done it without you. Finally, a huge thanks to my husband for working hard on this project with me, listening to me late at night explaining ideas, and for being my best friend!

Kimberly Christensen 2007

For me, this book is the result of my interactions with several individuals. Specifically, I thank my first mentor Dr. Scott Sells, author of Parenting Your Out of Control Teenager: 7 steps to Reestablish Authority and Reclaim Love, for the kindness and direction he gave to me. I thank all of my other professors and classmates at Savannah State University. I thank Drs. Claudia Kritz, Stephen Henry and Catherine Miller of Portland, OR for their patience, supervision, and direction. I thank Julie and Kim, my DBT mentors, supervisors, and co-authors for their patience and time spent teaching me DBT. I thank Corbett Monica of Portland, OR, founder of Dual Diagnosis Anonymous and mentor for much of my understanding and treatment of mental health and chemical dependency. I thank my friends and family for all their support. I thank Tommie Nuesse for his consultation on skill training and application techniques with children and adolescents. I thank Tory Sottile for all the technical assistance he has given me over the years. Most of all, I thank my companion for believing in me.

Gage Riddoch 2007

This has proven to be a path of excitement, set backs, and learning. I truly have valued working with my colleagues Gage Riddoch and Kim Christensen—two enthusiastic, dedicated, and skilled clinicians who move great ideas forward. Thank you both! I'd also like to thank my incredible parents who support my various endeavors with interest, encouragement, and great advice! They also taught me the importance of using one's WISE MIND and perseverance. Undoubtedly, my DBT mentors Bev Long, Psy.D. and Suzanne Witterholt, M.D are to be thanked for their unrelenting support of my interest and development in DBT. Their energy and incredible intelligence of this therapy/treatment has always inspired me to try harder. Thank you both! I would also like to acknowledge and thank my fellow wonderful DBT consultation team members who have worked so hard to learn and implement DBT practices-with great results. You all have been great supports and sources of inspiration. Thanks to you all. And most importantly, thank you to all the impressive clients I have been fortunate to work with over the years. Thank you for challenging me in ways to promote growth and for often showing me the way. And lastly, thanks my fabulous four legged family members who keep me balanced. You bring me joy and make life worth living.

Julie Eggers Huber 2007

Introduction

The themes and ideas in this book are the product of three clinicians practicing Dialectical Behavior Therapy (DBT) and seeking to broaden, assist, and facilitate the DBT learning experience for individuals of all ages, but especially for children and adolescents. Having worked in a combination of outpatient, inpatient, private, forensic, educational, and other treatment settings, we saw the need for a supplement to aid children and adolescents in learning new skills that can increase adaptive behaviors and overall behavior functioning. We quickly realized that presenting the skills in a more user-friendly way also helped adults, parents, teachers, and other clinicians to better understand and apply DBT skills and techniques.

Marsha Linehan[1] originally designed Dialectical Behavior Therapy for female adults struggling with self-harm and suicidal behaviors, by modifying components of Cognitive Behavior Therapy, and then adding elements of Zen wisdom and mindfulness practice. DBT is based on the idea that some people, due to invalidating environments during upbringing and due to biological factors still being researched, react abnormally to emotional stimulation. Their level of arousal goes up much more quickly, peaks at a higher level, and takes more time to return to baseline. This may explain why individuals with these problems are known for experiencing more crises than others, and tend to be more emotionally unstable. Because of their past invalidation, they don't have adequate methods for coping with these sudden, intense surges of emotion. DBT is a method for teaching coping and social skills that will help these individuals improve their lives. What is even more exciting is that now DBT appears to be effective for treating both youth and adults struggling with self-harm, suicide, suicidal ideations, non-suicidal self-injurious behaviors, depression, anxiety, post-traumatic stress disorder, bipolar disorder, chemical dependency, eating disorders, anger, relationships, and even low self-esteem!

Although DBT has some fabulous ideas and techniques, we have made several clinical observations and have received a lot of feedback from youth, parents, and other clinicians. We were told that the skills are often worded in a way that makes it difficult for children and adolescents to understand. Quite simply, at this point the therapy is still being adapted for children and adolescents, and sometimes lab researchers and other authors forget that not all individuals have their wide range of vocabulary or expert knowledge of therapeutic techniques. The fact is, a majority of the counselors in inpatient programs and a large number of support staff in other programs do not have graduate degrees in mental health. We believe more people should be able to teach or learn the DBT skills, thus improving the quality of their life and the lives of those they interact with by learning and understanding these skills in a fun and interactive way. Therefore, we have arranged each of the DBT skills in a straightforward and easily readable manner that allows a greater number of people an opportunity to start with the basics of the DBT skills, and then experience fun new ways to assist in learning and using these skills. This workbook is meant to be a supplement, and not a substitute for a comprehensive skills training workbook. In fact, we recommend you use this book as an introduction to learning and using DBT skills, or within a clinical setting as a supplement to Marsha Linehan's[3] Skills Training Manual for Treating Borderline Personality Disorder. We also highly recommend that individuals or clinicians seeking to work with this population adhere to the strictest of training standards, such as the Intensive Training provided by Behavior Tech, LLC as sponsored by Marsha Linehan and her training teams. Information about additional training and Behavior Tech, LLC can be found at www.behavioraltech.com.

In this workbook we have included the most comprehensive list of mindfulness exercises currently available within a workbook. We have also included many fun games and interactive learning aids that have helped many individuals learn and remember the DBT skills. In addition, you will find helpful templates for progress or group completion certificates, behavior coupons, and diary cards for monitoring behavior.

We know from experience that individuals of all ages are more likely to increase their effort and participation towards learning the DBT skills if they are engaged, having fun, feel challenged, and enjoy what they are doing. We know that it can be hard for some people to pay attention in long skill training groups, and we also know it is difficult to be angry, upset, or sad when you are having fun and enjoying what you are learning. When used correctly as a supplemental aid for learning the DBT skills, this learning supplement can broaden your DBT experience. We hope you enjoy our additional ideas we have shared with you here.

Gage Riddoch

Part I: DBT Skills

Before you can start using Dialectical Behavior Therapy (DBT) skills, you will need to know the content and application of each skill. Luckily, these skills have been arranged in ways that makes them easy to learn and even memorize if you want. An acronym is a word in which each letter of that word starts a new word. This arrangement makes it easier for you to categorize and remember more coping skills. We did not design these skills, but we can share them with you in a way that will benefit you.

Basically, the people who designed DBT[1] organized several coping methods into groups of coping skills specifically designed to assist individuals struggling with a number of problems related to relationships, emotional regulation, and other healthy functioning on a daily basis. A coping skill can be viewed as a positive way of handling or reacting to something that affects you in a negative way.

The skills we are going to share with you are part of a treatment approach called Dialectical Behavior Therapy (DBT). Similar to other people teaching these skills[2], we have taken the DBT skills and arranged them in a way that makes it easy for children, adolescents, and even adults to remember, understand, and use these skills. In the next section of this book there are skill summaries that can be used in skill training groups; as part of a worksheet or homework assignment; or the skills can be made into flashcards with the important parts of the skills on the back of the page in order to help you remember the skills. The first part of each skill is intended for the learner, and the teaching points on the back of each skill are intended for the teacher, staff, or parent assisting the learner. Following each skill module, there is a competency test for the individual skills. These quizzes are not official DBT tests, but many people find them very helpful. The answers to each quiz will be on the page following each skill module.

Once you learn the skills, you can use them at home, work, school, or any other time that it might help.

The five skill modules are Core Mindfulness, Walking the Middle Path, Distress Tolerance, Emotion Regulation, and Interpersonal Effectiveness. Within the Emotion Regulation module, we have added a skill called "Build Daily STRENGTH". This skill is not a DBT skill, but is similar to other DBT skills and can be very helpful. No matter who you are, there is a really good chance that if you learn these skills, you can feel better about yourself and improve the quality of your life.

Core Mindfulness

Core mindfulness skills are the foundation to learning DBT. The importance of mindfulness can be seen throughout all the other DBT skill modules. To be effective in implementing all DBT skills one must be able to mindfully focus their attention and be in control of their mind. As the authors of DBT[3] explain, there are three states of mind: reasonable mind, emotional mind, and wise mind. The goal is to be able to identify and understand the various states of mind, because the balance and integration of the different states of mind is very important. To help you balance the different states of mind, the "what" skills and the "how" skills were invented[3]. The "what" skills facilitate the ability to effectively observe, describe, and participate fully in one's experience. The "how" skills create the ability and awareness to be non-judgmental, stay focused in the moment, and do what works for the situation. The ultimate goal is to integrate one's emotional mind and reasonable mind; which will help you get to wise mind. Mindfulness skills can help you pay attention more at school or work, and can help you deal with anger or other types of emotions that may distract you from happiness. When you are mindful, you will find that learning and using the other skills in this book becomes a lot easier!

CORE MINDFULNESS

REASONABLE MIND

+

EMOTION MIND

=

WISE MIND

- **<u>Reasonable mind:</u>** is when your school brain is in control. Use your brain power, be a scientist. Remember cause and effect! A robot has all reason and no emotion.
- **<u>Emotion mind:</u>** is when your heart is in control; your feelings rule your behaviors. Emotions are important, as they don't control you.
- **<u>Wise mind</u>**: is a combination of reasonable mind and emotion mind. A harmony of heart and mind. This is the mixture we want to strive for.

Learning Points

Module: Core Mindfulness
Skill: States of Mind

Purpose of skill: Use the skill states of mind to assist individuals in gaining control of their own mind; this will decrease vulnerability to emotions.

Most important part of skill: There are three states of mind emotion mind, reasonable mind, and wise mind. Wise mind is the synthesis of emotion mind and reasonable mind.

Learning Strategies: Discuss times when you would be in emotional mind. Discuss times when you would be in reasonable mind. Describe the experience of being in wise mind and how you would know you are in wise mind.

Use this space to list things you already do that are similar to this skill and may have worked for you in the past. Or, write down any new ideas you have that we may have missed!

Notes: _____

_____

_____

_____

_____

_____

_____

_____

_____

_____

_____

_____

_____

_____

CORE
MINDFULNESS

WISE MIND <u>WHAT</u> SKILLS

OBSERVE:

Be a magnifying glass; look closely inside and outside of yourself. Be aware. Be a detective. Hold off on verbalizing what you see until you have taken it all in.

DESCRIBE:

Be a dictionary; name your experiences. Keep it simple and kind! Put it into words.

PARTICIPATE:

Like playing games; dive in. Action! Be actively involved. Experience your emotions. Don't let the moment pass you by. Help others to participate too!

Learning Points

Module: Core Mindfulness
Skill: WHAT skills

Purpose of skill: Use the WHAT skills to practice effectively "what to do" to engage in the core mindfulness skills.

Most important part of skill: Center your mind and body in each moment. Gain the ability to connect with your experience.

Learning Strategies: Role play each of the specific components of the WHAT skills. Discuss factors that get in the way of effectively observing, describing, and participating. Explain how the core mindfulness skills, specifically the WHAT skills, provide the foundation to effectively apply the other DBT skills. Remember, role play means to act out the situation.

Use this space to list things you already do that are similar to this skill and may have worked for you in the past. Or, write down any new ideas you have that we may have missed!

Notes: _____

_____

_____

_____

_____

_____

_____

_____

_____

_____

_____

_____

_____

CORE
MINDFULNESS
WISE MIND <u>HOW</u> SKILLS

Non-Judgmentally:
Stay away from name calling, teasing, or put downs. Use facts. Opinions can distract you from your ability to focus.

One Mindfully:
Pay attention to the moment you are in. Focus only on the task at hand. Clear your mind of everything else. It takes practice. Start simple, like with a single thought.

DO WHAT WORKS:
Make healthy and safe choices and the situation will work for you. Success! It helps to think about all the things that have worked in the past. There is a good chance those same things might work again now!

Learning Points

Module: Mindfulness
Skill: HOW Skills

Purpose of skill: These skills provide the "how" to be mindful.

Most important part of skill: Focus your mind. Tune out distractions. You are in charge of your mind.

Learning Strategies: Discuss how these skills make you mindful. Outline which of the HOW skills is most difficult for you and why. Discuss how being nonjudgmental may be similar to validation.

Use this space to list things you already do that are similar to this skill and may have worked for you in the past. Or, write down any new ideas you have that we may have missed!

Notes: _____

_____

_____

_____

_____

_____

_____

_____

_____

_____

_____

_____

_____

_____

Core Mindfulness Module Quiz

Name: _____   Date: _____

1. List the three states of mind:

   _____

   _____

   _____

2. Mindfulness should only be practiced one time daily. True or False

3. The HOW skills include: (circle all that apply)
   A. Non-Judgmentally
   B. Observe
   C. Participate
   D. One Mindfully

4. What does Observe mean within the WHAT skills?

   _____

   _____

5. List 3 times when you might be in emotion mind:

   _____

   _____

   _____

6. List 3 times when you might be in reasonable mind:

   _____

   _____

   _____

7. Describe wise mind.

   _____

   _____

   _____

8. List the WHAT skills:

   _____

   _____

   _____

9. Components of core mindfulness can be used in other DBT skills. True or False

10. To participate means to become one with your experience. True or False

Core Mindfulness Module Quiz-Answer Sheet

Name: _____   Date: _____

1. List the three states of mind:
   Emotional Mind
   Reasonable Mind
   Wise Mind

2. Mindfulness should only be practiced one time daily. True or **False**

3. The HOW skills include: (circle all that apply)
   a. **Non-Judgmentally**
   b. Observe
   c. Participate
   d. **One Mindfully**

4. What does Observe mean within the WHAT skills?
   Notice your experience; watch your thoughts and feelings coming and going.

5. List 3 times when you might be in emotion mind:
   Individualized answers; examples: during a funny movie, when you are in love, reading a romantic book, etc.

6. List 3 times when you might be in reasonable mind:
   Individualized answers; examples: in school, during an exam, reading a map, cooking a recipe, etc.

7. Describe wise mind.
   Individualized answers; example: The integration of emotional mind and reasonable mind.

8. List the WHAT skills:
   Observe, Describe, Participate

9. Components of core mindfulness can be used in other DBT skills. **True** or False

10. To participate means to become one with your experience. **True** or False

Walking the Middle Path

    Walking the Middle Path[2] was added to the DBT coping skills[3] to help people balance the ideas of acceptance and change. This skill group incorporates the concepts of dialectics, validation, and behaviorism. Dialectics assist in highlighting the significance of multiple points of view, creates movement toward "both/and" thinking and emphasizes the importance of recognizing change as the only constant. The concept of validation facilitates the development of active listening and tolerating others; in addition, it teaches children, adolescents, and their parents/caregivers how to validate themselves and each other by observing and describing current emotions and acknowledging such emotions as real, even if they are irrational. Behaviorism aids in promoting change in behaviors through reinforcement, shaping, and extinction of maladaptive behaviors; and increasing healthy and effective use of DBT coping strategies. What this means is that people should not try to focus too much on either change or acceptance, but that a balance between the two is the best fit when focusing on improving one's life circumstances. The ability to balance the ideas of change and acceptance can benefit any person regardless of your age or the problems you are faced with.

WALKING THE MIDDLE PATH

THINKING AND ACTING DIALECTICALLY

HINTS FOR FINDING THE MIDDLE PATH

1. Open your eyes to seeing things from many different angles. Often, there are many ways to solve a problem. Don't be afraid to research other solutions and see how other people in your situation may have solved their problem.

2. Nothing stays the same; change will happen. If what you are experiencing now is stressful, keep in mind that very few things remain the same. Change is constant.

3. Use "both/and" when viewing a situation or problem. Try to experiment with the "gray area" of things. Avoid black and white thinking and extremes, like "all or nothing", or "my way or the highway".

4. Remember the middle path is between acceptance and change. It is a balance. It requires both to be effective.

Learning Points

Module: Walking the Middle Path
Skill: Thinking & Acting Dialectically

Purpose of skill: Use dialectics to practice recognizing the various perspectives of things and numerous paths to problem solve. Use dialectics to facilitate flexibility in thinking and acting.

Most important part of skill: Consider all options. Avoid absolutes. Use flexible thinking.

Learning Strategies: Discuss a current dialectical dilemma you are experiencing and process the dilemma in terms of both/and or find the middle path. Provide information about the common dialectical dilemmas (emotional vulnerability, self-invalidation, active passivity, apparent competence, inhibited emotional experiencing, and unrelenting crises) and discuss which dilemmas you experience most often.

Use this space to list things you already do that are similar to this skill and may have worked for you in the past. Or, write down any new ideas you have that we may have missed!

Notes: _____
_____
_____
_____
_____
_____
_____
_____
_____
_____
_____
_____
_____

WALKING THE MIDDLE PATH

VALIDATE SELF

SOFTLY COMFORT YOURSELF BY RECOGNIZING WHAT YOU FEEL INSIDE AS IMPORTANT AND AS MAKING SENSE UNDER THE CURRENT CONDITIONS.

1. Tell yourself that what you feel is real, even when others don't understand. Nobody knows how you feel like you do. You can be the expert on you!
2. Don't expect others to know how you feel. After you understand and recognize that your feelings are genuine and real, you can better deal with those feelings and communicate those feelings to others.

Learning Points

Module: Walking the Middle Path
Skill: Validate Self

Purpose of Skill: Use the skill validate self to quietly reassure yourself that what you are experiencing and/or feeling is important and makes sense.

Most important part of skill: To provide acknowledgement to yourself and to understand your own experience.

Learning Strategies: Role-play validating self by practicing a non-judgmental stance, describing only the facts, and noticing what is valid about your experience. Discuss ways that you invalidate yourself; then list ways you could validate those invalidating experiences/comments. Discuss how to acknowledge and assess irrational or negative thoughts you experience. Practice just acknowledging that you are experiencing irrational or negative thoughts. List factors/situations/emotions/thoughts that can lead to invalidating thinking or behaviors. Talk about the importance of self validation for coping effectively, self-care, and self-esteem.

Use this space to list things you already do that are similar to this skill and may have worked for you in the past. Or, write down any new ideas you have that we may have missed!

Notes: _____

_____

_____

_____

_____

_____

_____

_____

_____

_____

_____

_____

WALKING THE MIDDLE PATH

VALIDATE OTHERS

1. Observe the experience. Mindfulness skills can be very helpful with this opportunity.

2. Describe the behavior you see with facts. This may help other people avoid blaming themselves.

3. Remember validation does not equal agreement or approval. Know what to validate, and what not to validate. It is helpful to assist other people with recognizing that feelings are real, but it may not be helpful to validate certain risky or unhealthy behaviors.

4. Validation is simply telling someone that you "get" what they feel or think under the current conditions!

Learning Points

Module: Walking the Middle Path
Skill: Validate someone else

Purpose of the skill: Use the skill validate others by observing the current experience and describing non-judgmentally the facts; focus on the person's inherent worth, the unstated feelings, and/or what is valid about the person's experience.

Most important part of skill: Be non-judgmental and acknowledge what the other person is experiencing.

Learning Strategies: Role-play validating someone else and listen to feedback from the other person regarding the validation you provided. Discuss the different types of validation that can be offered to someone. Describe how you have felt when someone has validated you and describe how they validated you. List factors that could be invalidating to you.

Use this space to list things you already do that are similar to this skill and may have worked for you in the past. Or, write down any new ideas you have that we may have missed!

Notes: _____

_____
_____
_____
_____
_____
_____
_____
_____
_____
_____
_____
_____

Walking the Middle Path Module Quiz

Name: _____   Date: _____

1. Thinking dialectically stresses the importance of black or white thinking. True or False

2. Change is the only thing that is constant. True or False

3. Who can you validate?

   _____

   _____

4. Validation means approval. True or False

5. Validation means:
   A. Approval
   B. Acknowledging what you feel
   C. Agreement
   D. Judging Others

6. Write out a validating statement about yourself at this moment:

   _____

   _____

   _____

7. Only you have the absolute truth. True or False

8. List 2 words you should avoid when thinking and acting dialectically:

   _____

   _____

9. Two things that appear opposite can both be true. True or False

10. Patients can fail in DBT. True or False

Walking the Middle Path Module Quiz-Answer Sheet

Name: _____   Date: _____

1. Thinking dialectically stresses the importance of black or white thinking. True or **False**

2. Change is the only thing that is constant. **True** or False

3. Who can you validate?
   Yourself & Someone Else

4. Validation means approval. True or **False**

5. Validation means:
   a. Approval
   b. Acknowledging what you feel
   c. Agreement
   d. Judging Others

6. Write out a validating statement about yourself at this moment:
   Individualized answers; example: "I am feeling nervous because I am taking this quiz."

7. Only you have the absolute truth. True or **False**

8. List 2 words you should avoid when thinking and acting dialectically:
   Individualized answers; examples: always, never, nobody, everyone, etc.

9. Two things that appear opposite can both be true. **True** or False

10. Patients can fail in DBT. True or **False**

Distress Tolerance

Many of the approaches in therapy to stressful and highly arousing situations involve learning skillful avoidance or modifying the circumstances. The goals of the DBT distress tolerance module are to teach children and adolescents how to effectively tolerate the distress and work through the moment. This module is significant because many times in life painful emotions or situations will be unavoidable. As a result of circumstances being unavoidable it is important that children, adolescents, and other individuals learn to accept distress and tolerate the moment. It is important that a variety of skills are learned to effectively manage diverse events and various emotions that one will encounter. There are several helpful acronyms[3] to remember a variety of strategies to effectively tolerate distress they include distracting with ACCEPTS, IMPROVE the Moment, Self-Soothe with the five senses, thinking in pros and cons, accepting reality through half-smile, and radical acceptance. These skills can be used at any time but are often used when someone is feeling unsafe, or when things just seem out of control in our lives or all around us. Sometimes when things get so bad, these skills seem to work better than some of the other coping skills in this book. Then, when the stressful moment is no longer unbearable, the other skill groups can also be very helpful to maintain the progress that these skills have helped you achieve.

DISTRESS TOLERANCE

DISTRACT YOURSELF WITH: "ACCEPTS"

Activities — Do an activity to keep your mind busy. Do something you enjoy, such as drawing, writing, or listening to music.

Contributing — Help others. Engage in a service project.

Comparison — Remind yourself about all the good things in your life. Take a moment to consider the things that are going well.

With opposite **E**motions: — Do something to create a different emotion than what you are currently feeling. Replace negatives with positives.

With **P**ushing Away: — Push the experience out of your mind for a bit. Some problems are handled better after the storm has passed.

With other **T**houghts: — Get active with other healthy thoughts and actions. You have more control over your thoughts than you may think.

With intense Other **S**ensations: — Excite your mind with intense safe sensations. Put a piece of ice in your hand, or take a cold shower.

Learning Points

Module: Distress Tolerance
Skill: Distract yourself with ACCEPTS

Purpose of skill: When things get stressful or difficult, these actions distract or keep your mind on getting through the moment and staying safe. The skills keep the mind focused on positive thoughts to cope through the situation.

Most important part of skill: Hard times pass—get through the moment.

Learning Strategies: Outline which parts of the skill are helpful when you are upset and why. Talk about the benefits of getting through hard times and likely outcomes. Identify five examples of strong sensations that are safe to use.

Use this space to list things you already do that are similar to this skill and may have worked for you in the past. Or, write down any new ideas you have that we may have missed!

Notes: _____

_____

_____

_____

_____

_____

_____

_____

_____

_____

_____

_____

_____

DISTRESS
TOLERANCE

SELF-SOOTHE

USE YOUR 5 SENSES TO COMFORT SELF & MANAGE DISTRESS EFFECTIVELY

With Vision: Watch a funny movie, check out the sunset, look at your old pictures, take in the scenery, or just close your eyes for a while.

With Hearing: Listen to your favorite music, listen to what people around you are saying, listen to what you are saying.

With Smell: Identify your favorite scent, smell the flowers, bake something that smells good, light some incense or a nice scented candle.

With Taste: Have a little of your favorite treat, try a new flavor of ice cream, make some hot chocolate, or just eat something sweet.

With Touch: Apply some lotion. Pet your favorite stuffed animal or the family dog. Use a stress ball. Paint your fingernails. Give someone a hug.

Learning Points

Module: Distress Tolerance
Skill: Self-Soothe

Purpose of skill: Use the skill self-soothe by using your five senses to comfort, nurture, be gentle, and regulate your mood during stressful situations.

Most important part of skill: Use core mindfulness to effectively self-soothe using your 5 senses.

Learning Strategies: List several ways to self-soothe for each of your 5 senses. Discuss times when using self-soothe would be helpful and effective. List factors that may get in the way of your abilities to self-soothe; develop a plan to manage the listed factors. Describe how the core mindfulness skills interact with the self-soothe skill.

Use this space to list things you already do that are similar to this skill and may have worked for you in the past. Or, write down any new ideas you have that we may have missed!

Notes: _____

_____

_____

_____

_____

_____

_____

_____

_____

_____

_____

_____

DISTRESS TOLERANCE

PROS & CONS

* **Focus on long-term goals:** It is easier to make progress when you are able to identify what it is you want to work on. It is easy to get caught up on the problem of the day and forget about the bigger things that help define you. Put your goal in writing in a place where you can see it everyday.

* **Think of all the good and bad reasons to make it through the situation:** Determine what your motivation is for wanting to endure whatever stress you are facing. Make a list and write it down so you can see it all in front of you and visualize all your options.

* **Think of all the good and bad reasons to *not* make it through the situation:** Ask yourself what you stand to benefit or lose if you decide not to endure the stress you are facing.

* **Remember to use your wise mind when making your choices:** Review your list, review the other skills you know, research the options, and then choose the best solution.

Learning Points

Module: Distress Tolerance
Skill: Pros & Cons

Purpose of skill: Use Pros & Cons to think about the positive and negative effects of accepting your current stress and the positive and negative effects of not accepting your current stress. Focus on long term goals; think of the positive results of accepting your current stress to reach long term goals.

Most important part of skill: Impulse control and focus on long-term goals.

Learning Strategies: List and then discuss the pros & cons of a current dilemma that you are experiencing. List times when this skill would be beneficial to use in your life. List factors that may get in the way of the pros & cons skill being effective. Discuss how to use the core mindfulness skills when developing a pros & cons list. Do it at a time when you are in wise mind, not when in a crisis or having high urges.

Use this space to list things you already do that are similar to this skill and may have worked for you in the past. Or, write down any new ideas you have that we may have missed!

Notes: _____
_____
_____
_____
_____
_____
_____
_____
_____
_____
_____
_____
_____

DISTRESS TOLERANCE

IMPROVE THE MOMENT

With **Imagery:** Imagine something relaxing or soothing. Think about your favorite memory or place. We are telling you to daydream!

With **Meaning:** Think of the important things in your life. What can be learned from difficult times? Have you survived anything like this before?

With **Prayer:** Pray, meditate, ponder, or just use your spirituality.

With **Relaxation:** Practice calming routines. Breathe. Breathe deeper. Allow events to unfold.

With **One thing in the moment:** Be aware of what you are doing now. Focus on just one thing at a time to avoid complications.

With a brief **Vacation:** Take a break. Exit for a while.

With **Encouragement:** Make helpful statements about yourself. Make helpful statements about others.

Learning Points

Module: Distress Tolerance
Skill: IMPROVE

Purpose of skill: These skills work to create positive thoughts and an even mood allowing someone to get through a difficult time.

Most important part of skill: Meditation practices work.

Learning Strategies: Discuss how this skill is similar to ACCEPTS. Identify what your favorite IMPROVE skills are and why. Explain why IMPROVE activities help someone feel better. Provide some examples of IMPROVE activities that you use. Discuss why it is important to use and practice these when you aren't stressed out.

Use this space to list things you already do that are similar to this skill and may have worked for you in the past. Or, write down any new ideas you have that we may have missed!

Notes: _____
_____
_____
_____
_____
_____
_____
_____
_____
_____
_____
_____
_____
_____

DISTRESS TOLERANCE

HALF SMILE

Here's how to do it:

Make your lips smile a little and relax the muscles in your face. Try to make your face calm. Accept the situation you are in by half-smiling. Your body talks to your brain and can change your emotions on the inside by changing what you do on the outside.

A half smile helps you get through the moment. It does not involve sarcasm. It can be sincere. It can be brief or last a long time. It is a simple exercise that can help you manage something stressful.

Learning Points

Module: Distress Tolerance
Skill: Half-Smile

Purpose of skill: Changing our body and face can help change our mood.

Most important part of skill: Relax your face as you practice this skill. Heads up, the body speaks to the mind!

Learning Strategies: Talk about what makes this a Crisis Survival Skill. List ways this skill may be similar to Opposite Action. Outline why this skill often makes us feel better. Debate whether or not this skill helps turn the mind.

Use this space to list things you already do that are similar to this skill and may have worked for you in the past. Or, write down any new ideas you have that we may have missed!

Notes: _____

_____
_____
_____
_____
_____
_____
_____
_____
_____
_____
_____
_____
_____

DISTRESS TOLERANCE

RADICAL ACCEPTANCE

<u>Basic Principles of Accepting Reality</u>

- **Life can be tough:** The sooner you understand that life is not always fair or easy, the better you will be able to accept things that are out of your control.

- **Some things cannot be changed:** Try to agree or at least admit that there are some things we cannot change. This can help you focus on the things that can change.

- **It is what it is…** The idea that you can accept certain unchangeable things and balance those things with what you can change will help you get though the moment.

- **You may not always agree or like it:** Of course we like to have things work out the way we want them too. That is human nature. That is not always possible. Agree to disagree.

Learning Points

Module: Distress Tolerance
Skill: Radical Acceptance

Purpose of skill: Use radical acceptance to remove yourself from struggling against reality when you cannot keep painful events, emotions, and life circumstances from coming your way.

Most important part of skill: Keep in mind some things cannot be changed. Some things must be accepted; radical acceptance is not approval, and can be a tough process.

Learning Strategies: Discuss areas in your life where you could use the skill radical acceptance. List emotions and other factors that get in the way of accepting reality. Describe ways you can accept reality with the assistance of other DBT skills.

Use this space to list things you already do that are similar to this skill and may have worked for you in the past. Or, write down any new ideas you have that we may have missed!

Notes: _____

_____

_____

_____

_____

_____

_____

_____

_____

_____

_____

_____

_____

_____

Distress Tolerance Module Quiz

Name: _____   Date: _____

1. What skill uses your five senses?
    A. ACCEPTS
    B. IMPROVE
    C. Self-Soothe
    D. Half-Smile

2. Pros and cons mean looking at only what you can get from a situation. True or False

3. What does the I stand for in IMPROVE?
    _____

4. List 5 Activities you can do to distract yourself with ACCEPTS.
    _____
    _____
    _____
    _____
    _____

5. With Encouragement in the skill IMPROVE means to make helpful statements about yourself. True or False

6. Distress tolerance skills can help you through the moment. True or False

7. Name a distress tolerance skill and how you have used it.
    _____
    _____
    _____

8. What does the P stand for in ACCEPTS?
    _____

9. A half-smile is a tense grin. True or False

10. Radical acceptance means approval of what is currently happening. True or False

Distress Tolerance Module Quiz-Answer Sheet

Name: _____   Date: _____

1. What skill uses your five senses?
    a. ACCEPTS
    b. IMPROVE
    c. Self-Soothe
    d. Half-Smile

2. Pros and cons mean looking at only what you can get from a situation. True or **False**

3. What does the I̲ stand for in IMPROVE?
    Imagery

4. List 5 A̲ctivities you can do to distract yourself with ACCEPTS.
    Individualized answers; examples: call a friend, ride your bike, watch a TV show, journal, read a book, etc.

5. Encouragement in the skill IMPROVE means to make helpful statements about yourself. **True** or False

6. Distress tolerance skills can help you through the moment. **True** or False

7. Name a distress tolerance skill and how you have used it.
    Individualized answers; example: "I used self-soothe with touch. I went home and held my kitten."

8. What does the P̲ stand for in ACCEPTS?
    With Pushing Away

9. A half-smile is a tense grin. True or **False**

10. Radical acceptance means approval of what is currently happening. True or **False**

Emotion Regulation

Many children and adolescents who struggle with mental illness have developed a high sensitivity to emotions, intense emotional experiences and a slow return to baseline. As a result of this combination many children and adolescents become easily dysregulated and require extended periods of time to return to a baseline level of emotional functioning. The emotion regulation skills[3] were intended to target development of the abilities to identify and label emotions accurately; accounting for primary and secondary emotional experiences. In addition, the emotion regulation skills teach children, adolescents, and other individuals the importance of their emotions in communicating to self/others, motivating action, and validating experiences. Within the Emotion Regulation module, we have added a skill called "Build Daily Strength". This skill is not a DBT skill, but is similar to other DBT skills and can be very helpful. Throughout this module we have highlighted reducing vulnerability to emotions through daily self-care, increasing daily positive experiences, incorporating mindfulness practices with current emotions, acting opposite to current emotion and utilizing distress tolerance strategies. You can control your emotions, and this group of skills makes it easier to identify which ways work best for you. Mastery of this group of skills can help you feel better about yourself.

EMOTION REGULATION

HOW TO STAY OUT OF EMOTIONAL MIND

Build Daily STRENGTH
(a non-DBT skill)

Balance Sleep: Practice healthy sleep habits.

Take Care of Self: Take care of your body.

Resist Target Behaviors: Avoid harmful activities.

Get Exercise: Exercise daily.

Balance Nutrition: Eat foods that are good for you.

Gain Mastery: Take charge once a day.

Take Time for Yourself: Do something fun daily.

Healthy Self-Talk: Say nice things about yourself.

Learning Points

Module: Emotion Regulation
Skill: Build Daily STRENGTH

Purpose of skill: Practicing healthy habits of daily living each day helps keep people emotionally regulated. Exercising, taking care of your body, eating right, not using illegal drugs or alcohol, sleeping well, and building self mastery (doing activities that make you feel competent) into daily practice.

Most important part of skill: Self-care is the key to keeping emotionally balanced.

Learning Strategies: Identify areas that might need more work for self-care and identify what you could do to make it better. Discuss why eating or sleeping poorly affects your mood. Outline your healthy habits and how they elevate your mood. Discuss why exercise often helps your feel better.

Use this space to list things you already do that are similar to this skill and may have worked for you in the past. Or, write down any new ideas you have that we may have missed!

Notes: _____
_____
_____
_____
_____
_____
_____
_____
_____
_____
_____
_____
_____

EMOTION REGULATION

BUILD UP DAILY POSITIVE EXPERIENCES

ENGAGE IN PLEASANT EVENTS

What do you like to do? Make your own list:

- Go swimming
- Exercise
- Watch a movie
- Call a friend
- Go for a walk
- Ride a bike
- Play a game
- Make something yummy to eat
- Go to the park
- Write in a journal or diary
- Organize your closet
- Go shopping
- Get your nails done
- Take a bubble bath
- Draw a picture or paint
- Listen to music
- Make music

Learning Points

Module: Emotion Regulation
Skill: Engage in Pleasant Activities

Purpose of skill: Build up positive experiences to feel better and make life worth living. Use mindfulness skills to enjoy activities fully.

Most important part of skill: It is important to have fun, play, and enjoy yourself.

Learning Strategies: List five benefits to doing pleasant activities. Discuss why thinking about worries ruins fun events. Determine how often you need to do fun things.

Use this space to list things you already do that are similar to this skill and may have worked for you in the past. Or, write down any new ideas you have that we may have missed!

Notes: _____

_____

_____

_____

_____

_____

_____

_____

_____

_____

_____

_____

_____

EMOTION REGULATION

MINDFULNESS OF CURRENT EMOTION

- **Make friends with your emotions:** It is easier to manage your emotions if you can first identify how you are feeling. This takes practice at first. If you are not aware of your emotions, you are more likely to react first and think later.

- **Become skilled in knowing what emotion you are experiencing:** The more you practice, the quicker you will be able to identify your current emotion. The more you can identify your current emotion, the more skilled you will be at managing that emotion.

- **Use observe and describe:** The skills work well together, and sometimes emotions can be tricky. If you take a moment to observe you feelings and put it into words, you may find you are actually experiencing stress as opposed to anger, or concern as opposed to frustration, etc.

Learning Points

Module: Emotion Regulation
Skill: Mindfulness of Current Emotion

Purpose of skill: Becoming skilled at knowing your emotions and befriending them by mindfully experiencing emotions, reminding yourself that you are not your emotions, and knowing that experiencing emotions are natural and important.

Most important part of skill: Surf out the emotion—you will survive and the emotion will pass. Don't think about every other time you have felt this way.

Learning Strategies: Discuss how you learned about emotions and what were the lessons you were taught. Identify the scariest emotion for you and why. List three benefits to practicing this skill. Role-play experiencing some difficult news and how you might be mindful of your current emotion.

Use this space to list things you already do that are similar to this skill and may have worked for you in the past. Or, write down any new ideas you have that we may have missed!

Notes: _____
_____
_____
_____
_____
_____
_____
_____
_____
_____
_____
_____
_____
_____

EMOTION REGULATION

CHANGE EMOTIONS
by Acting Opposite to the Current Emotion

- First: Identify your current emotion by observing and describing.

- Second: If safe, move toward the upsetting problem, person, or emotion.

EXAMPLES:

Emotion	Urge	Opposite Action
Sad	Be Alone	Be around others
Angry	Yell or Attack	Be extra kind
Frustrated	Give up	Try even harder
Betrayed	Hurt or Revenge	Forgiveness
Worthless	Harm self	Help others

Learning Points

Module: Emotion Regulation
Skill: Opposite Action

Purpose of skill: Every emotion has an action or urge associated with it. A person can change their emotion by acting opposite to the current emotion. So, if you are sad and depressed, get active. If angry, be respectful and a bit kind. If scared, act brave and move toward situation (if it's safe to do so). If feeling shame, use cheerleading statements.

Most important part of skill: Just do it. Jump in.

Learning Strategies: Discuss how this skill might be similar to Half Smile. Debate whether or not using fake opposite action is still useful. List out your action urges for sadness, anger, fear, and shame, and then what the opposition action looks like for each one.

Use this space to list things you already do that are similar to this skill and may have worked for you in the past. Or, write down any new ideas you have that we may have missed!

Notes: _____

_____

_____

_____

_____

_____

_____

_____

_____

_____

_____

_____

_____

_____

Emotion Regulation Module Quiz

Name: _____   Date: _____

1. List 3 of the 8 primary emotions:
   _____
   _____
   _____

2. What is the opposite action to the emotion anger?
   _____
   _____

3. List the skill you use daily to keep out of emotional mind.
   _____

4. List 5 pleasant events you can put into your daily routine:
   _____
   _____
   _____
   _____
   _____

5. Observing and describing can assist with emotion identification. True or False

6. What does the S stand for in STRENGTH?
   A. Sleep as much as you can
   B. Stay focused
   C. Snack during the day
   D. Balance your sleep

7. Balanced eating is part of daily self-care within the STRENGTH skill. True or False

8. List one way you build self-mastery daily.
   _____

9. Acting opposite to current emotion means stuffing your current emotion inside. True or False

10. What does the E stand for in STRENGTH?
    A. Eat daily
    B. Exercise daily
    C. Exercise once a week
    D. Earn privileges

Emotion Regulation Module Quiz-Answer Sheet

Name: _____   Date: _____

1. List 3 of the 8 primary emotions:
    Anger, sorrow, joy, fear, disgust, guilt/shame, interest, surprise

2. What is the opposite action to the emotion anger?
    Gently avoid the person you are upset with; do something nice rather than mean; imagine sympathy and/or empathy for the person.

3. List the skill you use daily to keep out of emotional mind.
    STRENGTH

4. List 5 pleasant events you can put into your daily routine:
    Individualized answers; examples: play a game, take a bath, go for a walk, talk with a friend, watch the clouds, read a book, meditate, doodle, dance, etc.

5. Observing and describing can assist with emotion identification. **True** or False

6. What does the S stand for in STRENGTH?
    a. Sleep as much as you can
    b. Stay focused
    c. Snack during the day
    d. Balance your sleep

7. Balanced eating is part of daily self-care within the STRENGTH skill. **True** or False

8. List one way you build self-mastery daily.
    Answers will be individualized.

9. Acting opposite to current emotion means stuffing your current emotion inside. True or **False**

10. What does the E stand for in STRENGTH?
    a. Eat daily
    b. Exercise daily
    c. Exercise once a week
    d. Earn privileges

Interpersonal Effectiveness

Children, adolescents and other individuals who have difficulty creating healthy and effective relationships often struggle to achieve their objectives, keep current relationships and maintain their self-respect when attempting to obtain a specific outcome from a situation. Many times they will resort to aggressive or passive communication styles making it challenging for them to create and keep healthy relationships. The interpersonal effectiveness module attempts to target circumstances that call for healthy skill use, recognize situations that may reduce one's ability to use skills effectively, and assists with identification of ways to cheerlead or encourage self or others during interpersonal situations. In addition, this group of skills has several helpful acronyms targeting specific aspects of interpersonal interactions including DEAR MAN (objective effectiveness), GIVE (relationship effectiveness), and FAST (self-respect effectiveness)[3]. Basically, this group of skills can help you get along better with people in your relationships at work, home, and school.

INTERPERSONAL EFFECTIVENESS

CHEERLEADING STATEMENTS

- Cheerleading statements give us the courage to do things when times are tough: Anyone can lead be a leader or motivate oneself to do better or try harder.

- Cheerleading statements make you stronger and ready for action: Think about this as mental preparation or self-motivation. If you believe you can do it, then you can. If you have doubts, it may be difficult until you practice telling yourself it can work.

- Cheerleading statements can fight off untrue thoughts: Doubt can be reduced simply by telling yourself over and over again that you have the power to do something.

- "I am okay!"
- "I will be okay!"
- "I can do it!"
- "This is my choice!"
- "I am strong!"

Learning Points

Module: Interpersonal Effectiveness
Skill: Cheerleading Statements

Purpose of skill: Positive self-statements people make to give themselves permission to ask for what they need or want, to say no, or to give themselves courage or comfort.

Most important part of skill: Be kind to yourself. Keep your self talk positive.

Learning Strategies: Discuss why positive self talk is so important. Talk about the kind of self talk you might be using if you don't engage in cheerleading. Identify five additional benefits to using cheerleading statements. Role-play examples of cheerleading statements in a variety of tough situations.

Use this space to list things you already do that are similar to this skill and may have worked for you in the past. Or, write down any new ideas you have that we may have missed!

Notes: _____

_____

_____

_____

_____

_____

_____

_____

_____

_____

_____

_____

_____

_____

INTERPERSONAL EFFECTIVENESS

HOW TO GET SOMEONE TO DO WHAT YOU WANT

DEAR MAN

Describe: List the facts. Put it into words.

Express: Talk about your feelings. Say why you want what you want.

Assert: Say exactly what you want. Be able to accept a "no" sometimes.

Reinforce: Tell the other person what they will get out of the deal. Strengthen your request with previous examples and times that you followed through or kept your promise.

(be) **M**indful: Be focused. Don't be distracted by less meaningful details or arguments. A clear and calm approach presented mindfully is more likely to be accepted.

Appear Confident: Use a nice tone of voice. Look people in the eye. Speak clearly, and do not stammer or beat around the bush.

Negotiate: Discuss options. Be open to other suggestions and ideas. Be willing to give to get. Have other ideas in mind.

Learning Points

Module: Interpersonal Effectiveness
Skill: DEAR MAN

Purpose of skill: To effectively get what you want by talking and interacting in a kind and calm way.

Most important part of skill: Keep your cool when you talk with others. People are more likely to listen to you and then you will be more likely to get what you want.

Learning Strategies: Discuss how you can still get what you want when you negotiate. Identify why it is important to appear confident when interacting. List five reasons why when you say something in a mean way, it's unlikely you'll get what you want.

Use this space to list things you already do that are similar to this skill and may have worked for you in the past. Or, write down any new ideas you have that we may have missed!

Notes: _____

_____

_____

_____

_____

_____

_____

_____

_____

_____

_____

_____

_____

INTERPERSONAL EFFECTIVENESS

HOW TO KEEP A GOOD RELATIONSHIP

GIVE

(be) **Gentle:** Be nice and respectful. No fighting. Don't be a bully. Speak calmly and make nice comments.

(act) **Interested:** Listen to the other person. Make good eye contact. Don't make faces. Wait until the other person is done to talk.

Validate: Be aware of the other person's feelings and situation. Let them know what they are feeling is real.

(use an) **Easy Manner:** It's okay to be silly and laugh sometimes. Be friendly. Be approachable. Be open for advice.

Learning Points

Module: Interpersonal Effectiveness
Skill: GIVE

Purpose of skill: Use the GIVE skill to develop or keep healthy relationships in your life or to assist with ending harmful relationships.

Most important part of the skill: Focus on body language, voice tone, non-verbal communication, and the current relationship.

Learning Strategies: Discuss times when this skill would be helpful to use in your life. Discuss factors that may get in the way of the GIVE skill being effective. List ways people show they are interested in you and list ways you show others that you are interested in them. Role-play with someone the GIVE skill using a current relationship in your life you are developing, keeping, or attempting to end.

Use this space to list things you already do that are similar to this skill and may have worked for you in the past. Or, write down any new ideas you have that we may have missed!

Notes: _____
_____
_____
_____
_____
_____
_____
_____
_____
_____
_____
_____
_____

INTERPERSONAL EFFECTIVENESS

HOW TO KEEP YOUR SELF-RESPECT

FAST

(be) Fair: Treat others as you want to be treated. Remember the Golden Rule! Sometimes you win sometimes you lose, but balance what you take with what you give.

(no) Apologies: Don't say sorry for being you; apologize when you make a mistake. Don't over apologize.

Stick to Values: Remember what is important to you and what you believe in. You decide your actions, not anyone else.

(be) Truthful: Be honest. Take responsibility for your actions.

Learning Points

Module: Interpersonal Effectiveness
Skill: FAST

Purpose of skill: Use the FAST skill to gain mastery and self-respect by sticking to your values and beliefs and by being fair and honest.

Most important part of the skill: Be true to your values and beliefs in order to gain self-respect.

Learning Strategies: Discuss the values that build the foundation of your life. List ways you are working toward those values. Define the word apology. List times when it is appropriate to apologize. Have a discussion about ways you are gaining mastery in your life. Develop a plan to address barriers to gaining mastery if necessary. Role-play with someone the FAST skill to practice building self-respect with a current scenario that has been problematic for you.

Use this space to list things you already do that are similar to this skill and may have worked for you in the past. Or, write down any new ideas you have that we may have missed!

Notes: _____

_____

_____

_____

_____

_____

_____

_____

_____

_____

_____

_____

_____

Interpersonal Effectiveness Module Quiz

Name: _____   Date: _____

1. Which interpersonal effectiveness skill would you use if your goal was getting something you want?
   A. DEAR MAN
   B. GIVE
   C. ACCEPTS
   D. FAST

2. The <u>A</u> in DEAR MAN stands for argue your point until the other person agrees. True or False

3. What do the letters stand for in FAST?
   F _____
   A _____
   S _____
   T _____

4. The GIVE skill teaches you how to build/keep a good relationship. True or False

5. What skill teaches you how to build/keep your self-respect?
   A. IMPROVE
   B. Radical Acceptance
   C. FAST
   D. ACCEPTS

6. Interpersonal myths can be challenged with cheerleading statements. True or False

7. The <u>G</u> in GIVE stands for (be) Gentle. True or False

8. What does the <u>N</u> stand for in DEAR MAN?
   _____

9. Write one cheerleading statement you use.
   _____
   _____

10. The <u>I</u> in GIVE stands for interrupt often. True or False

Interpersonal Effectiveness Module Quiz-Answer Sheet

Name: _____ Date: _____

1. Which interpersonal effectiveness skill would you use if your goal was getting something you want?
   a. **DEAR MAN**
   b. GIVE
   c. ACCEPTS
   d. FAST

2. The <u>A</u> in DEAR MAN stands for argue your point until the other person agrees. True or **False**

3. What do the letters stand for in FAST?
   F **(be) Fair**
   A **(no) Apologies**
   S **Stick to Values**
   T **(be) Truthful**

4. The GIVE skill teaches you how to build/keep a good relationship. **True** or False

5. What skill teaches you how to build/keep your self-respect?
   a. IMPROVE
   b. Radical Acceptance
   c. **FAST**
   d. ACCEPTS

6. Interpersonal myths can be challenged with cheerleading statements. **True** or False

7. The <u>G</u> in GIVE stands for (be) Gentle. **True** or False

8. What does the <u>N</u> stand for in DEAR MAN?
   Negotiate

9. Write one cheerleading statement you use.
   Individualized answers; examples: "I can do it." "This won't last forever."

10. The <u>I</u> in GIVE stands for interrupt often. True or **False**

Part II: 101 Mindfulness Exercises

To be mindful means to be attentive and focused. It is important for many reasons. Being mindful helps us pay attention to our thoughts, feelings, behaviors, and much more. Mindfulness can be short or long, serious or silly, and can help us balance our emotions and lower our stress. Many people use mindfulness exercises for a lot of different reasons. Dialectical Behavior Therapy (DBT) mindfulness is similar to other mindfulness exercises. In addition, it can be very helpful for dealing with anger. The more we do mindfulness, the better we become at staying calm and focused. When adults do mindfulness exercises with children and adolescents, it can increase the level of trust between them and make communication much easier. Mindfulness can be done within individual and group settings. Many of our mindfulness exercises are a lot of fun, because we know people love to have fun. We couldn't possibly think of every mindfulness exercise available, so perhaps these ideas that we have collected will help you come up with even more exercises of your own!

You can be mindful all by yourself or in a group setting too. To be mindful on an individual basis we suggest using the Mindfulness skills in section 1 of this book. Most of the mindfulness exercises in this book are intended for group settings. Being mindful with others or conducting a mindfulness exercise in a group setting can be a wonderful and refreshing experience. First, a group leader or special group member introduces the exercise and how the other group members should participate, and then that person reminds the other group members to refocus if they find their minds wandering. Members are encouraged to participate using the DBT mindfulness skills learned in section 1 of this book. Then, members should be given an opportunity to share their sensations and emotions, and process the experience. For each exercise, an additional learning task may involve having members identify which aspects of the mindfulness skills in Part 1 of this book that they used, such as Observe, Describe, etc. It may be different for everyone involved, but these exercises will strengthen the effectiveness of all the other DBT skills. Here are some mindfulness exercises for you to try!

1. Mindfulness Story: Someone in the group initiates an opening line on a piece of paper and then passes the paper to the next group member. That group member reads the existing storyline to him or herself, and then has 1 minute to write an addition to the story before passing it on to the next group member, who then repeats the process until each group member has had a chance to participate. After the last group member has finished, that person or the group leader will then read the final story product. It is often very amusing. The opening line can be anything, but may read something like "After I got home from school today, the craziest thing happened. I opened the door to my bedroom and…" or "Just when I thought I was going to go crazy with boredom, I decided to…" or "I knew this was a good idea, taking a long vacation. I wonder where I will go…" or for younger children "I am thinking of something sweet to eat. Maybe I will eat…" This mindfulness exercise can also be done verbally with younger children.

2. Transformation: Each member is given an everyday object (examples: serving spoon, golf club, etc.); next they are asked to think creatively about the object they have received and are encouraged to be mindful of what other everyday use the object could be transformed into. Then they show and tell the group how they have transformed the object.

3. Rhythm Game: One member starts with a rhythm (clapping hands); then the next member claps their hands and adds an additional rhythm; this rhythm game continues through the entire group; starting over if someone forgets a rhythm.

4. Name Game: Group leader or other individual offers up a name, and each group member takes a turn coming up with a name that starts with the last letter of the name previously mentioned. This works for many categories, such as favorite musician/band, cities, cars, clothing brands, or even food!

5. Making the sound of a Rain Storm: The facilitator of the group starts by rubbing their hands together and each person follows copying the sound of the person next to them; once everyone is rubbing their hands and the sound returns to the facilitator, similar to a wave, the facilitator starts snapping their fingers and this motion goes around in a wave motion (people continue rubbing their hands together until the snapping motion reaches them); next the facilitator starts the same process by patting their legs again going around in a wave motion; then the facilitator stomps their feet in the same wave motion, following the process described above; next the facilitator pats her legs when the sound returns to them; then snaps their fingers

and ends with rubbing their hands together all in the motion of a wave, thus creating the sound of a rainstorm.

6. The Game of Telephone: Group leader or individual member whispers a brief message into the ear of the group member sitting directly next to him or her, and then the message is whispered and passed on around the group until back to the leader, who recites the message, which is often a completely new message.

7. Two Truths & a Lie: Group leader or member takes turns telling two truthful bits of information about themselves or other facts or general knowledge, mixed with an inaccurate statement that group members must guess as such. Each group member takes a turn.

8. Finger Painting: Each member is given some finger paint and allowed to finger paint on provided paper. Specific instructions can be provided about what to finger paint or the members can be allowed to just notice the sensations of the finger paint.

9. Lotion: Group members each apply a scented lotion, often from a choice of more than one kind, and inhales scent. Group members each share memories generated or give general feedback regarding the experience.

10. 3D Optical Illusions: Pictures of optical illusions are brought in by the facilitator or group members and everyone is asked to focus on the pictures and locate the optical illusions; or "see" the pictures that come out of the photos. A variation of this is to pass out sheets of paper filled with optical illusions (available online and in many books) and have group members unravel the mysteries together.

11. Small Stuffed Animal Pass: Group leader starts with one stuffed animal and passes it to the same person each time. Slowly at first and then more quickly additional animals are added in the same order, and group members continue to pass and catch from same person. Beanie Babies and small soft items work well. Remind the group members this is not dodge ball!

12. Color a picture with non-dominant hand. A variation is to write the alphabet with your non-dominant hand.

13. Complete a short maze: Mazes are usually available online or in small affordable books in many places. Each member is given a short maze and asked to focus on getting through the maze with minimal to no errors. Process the experience of the instructions.

14. Relaxation Strategies for the body: Squeeze out the lemon juice (hands), stretch like a cat (arms overhead), shrug your shoulders tight & go into your shell, bite down on bubble gum ball (clench your jaw), wrinkle your nose get the bug off your nose, tighten your stomach, the elephant may step on it, squish your toes in the mud, tighten your toes.

15. Mints, fruits (kiwi, apples, pineapple, oranges, etc.), juices (lemonade, raspberry juice, etc.), other types of candy (chocolates, lemon heads, fire balls, etc.): Group members are instructed to simultaneously place item in mouth and allow sensations to form. One minute is usually a good amount of time for mints and other candies and members are instructed not to actually bite into candy once inside mouth until one minute has passed.

16. List all the songs you know with _____ word in the title.

17. List as many foods as you can that start with the letter _____.

18. List as many types of _____ movies.

19. Write the words to your favorite song.

20. Draw how your heart feels: Give each member paper and markers; encourage them to draw how their heart feels in the moment or with words describe how their heart feels in the moment.

21. Create your special place (follow guidelines): Creating a place for relaxation and guidance; this place can be inside or outside; allow private entry into your place; make it peaceful, comfortable, and safe; fill your place with sensuous details and create all the details of what your "special place" looks, feels, and sounds like.

22. Self-hug: Have each member wrap their arms tightly around themselves and squeeze tightly.

23. Play three rounds of "duck duck goose" with group members.

24. Suitcase: Have group members be mindful of all the people, places, things, values, etc. that are important to them, and then have them place these things in their "life suitcase".

25. Have group members share all the ways they receive pleasure, comfort, and/or enjoyment through each of your five senses.

26. Have group members sit back to back in pairs and describe the drawing they have on their paper to their partner who will attempt to draw what they are being told without seeing the drawing. Then, switch roles.

27. Candy Necklace: have group members mindfully string a necklace made of lifesavers or candy with holes. At the end of the group members get to eat the candy.

28. Read a poem or short story (i.e. Chicken Soup for the Soul books).

29. Group members write personal worries, fears, troubles, etc. on a small piece of paper; then put all pieces of paper in a hat; next each member draws out a piece of paper and reads the personal worry, fear, trouble, etc., and describes how the member might feel. This mindfulness helps members practice validation and empathy.

30. Play Musical Chairs: Age-old game of advancing to the empty chair when music stops. Last group member in a chair has to lead the next mindfulness exercise.

31. Mandala Coloring: Find complex or unique mandala or mandala-like symbols and have members focus on coloring these complex and/or unique pictures.

32. Sounds of Nature: Go outside and listen to the surrounding sounds for 1 minute writing down all the different sounds heard for 1 minute.

33. Create a collage of emotions: Using magazines, markers, stickers, and other creative materials to create a collage of one emotion or various emotions each member is feeling at the time of the exercise.

34. Mind Teasers: Find a book of mind teasers/benders and have members guess the answers and/or be mindful of the complexity of them.

35. Play Dough: Give each group member one color of play dough or several different colors of play dough and have them build their current emotion. Or have them depict "wise mind."

36. Put objects (ball, fruit, keys, rock, coin, piece of leather, etc.) in a small box and have group members feel in the box and guess the objects.

37. Repeat exercise #36 but this time have the group members wear gloves.

38. Squeeze a piece of white paper and have group members look for objects/pictures. A variation is to go outside and look for pictures in the clouds.

39. Chair Sit: Have group members sit with their back against a wall and then move into a chair position with body. Have members notice the sensations in their legs.

40. Jelly Beans: Bring in a variety of different flavors of jelly beans and have people guess the flavors or announce the flavors and have group members be mindful of the taste and the flavor it resembles.

41. My Orange: Place several oranges in a bowl; then have each member pick out an orange; next have members be mindful of the orange they have chosen and the markings of their orange; have everyone place their oranges back in the bowl; lastly have each member find their orange in the bowl of several oranges. This can be done with bananas, apples, leaves, etc.

42. Put rice/beans into a large bowl; then place a small object into the bowl and have group members search mindfully for the small object in the bowl.

43. Have group members put ice in their mouth and notice the feeling, or have group members put ice in their hand and notice the sensation.

44. "If" questions: Come up with a list of several "if" style questions and ask each member to answer the question (example: "If you had a million dollars what would you do?").

45. Skill Charades: Place several names of DBT skills in a container and then have each group member pick out a skill; then they need to act out the skill following agreed upon rules similar to charades; the group is mindful of observing and describing the skills.

46. Float Your Tongue: Have group members hold their tongue up and inside their mouth, not allowing their tongue to touch the bottom or sides of their mouth while keeping their mouth closed; notice the sensations felt in the body.

47. Essential Oils: Have group members rub oil on their temples and behind their ears, and educate group members as to which oils are designed for which purposes. Observe the sensations.

48. Light a candle and smell the scent. A variation is to have group members pass around an unlit candle and have them guess the scent if unknown.

49. Hot Chocolate/Apple Cider: Have group members sip hot chocolate or apple cider and notice the feelings that occur in their body; describe memories associated with the drinks.

50. Compassion for Others: Have each member silently be mindful about someone else in the room; encourage them to think about cheerleading thoughts and/or ways to provide validation to the person they are being mindful about.

51. Listen to a song or a clip of a song and allow group members to analyze content or emotions elicited from that media.

52. Look at pictures removed from a magazine and have each group member make up a story for that picture.

53. Have each group member state which animal they would be if they could be an animal, and explain why.

54. Have group members describe their favorite food without actually naming it, gradually giving up to three hints until another group member guesses correctly, making it that group member's turn to participate.

55. Have group members write themselves a letter one week in advance, and one week later have group leader deliver it to them in group to read aloud or process silently. Possible guidelines for content include using validating or cheerleading statements.

56. First Words: Pass around a pen or pencil and have the group members pretend it is a microphone, and then have each member imitate what they think their first words or sounds as a baby or small child might have been.

57. Automobile Assimilation: Have group members describe what type of car or truck they would be and explain why. For example, "I would be a tow truck because I usually help people when they are out of luck."

58. Self-portrait: Have group members draw themselves in one minute and present to group.

59. Play Stickman (a version of Hangman) using DBT skills as the letters and words that need to be guessed prior to completion of the stick man.

60. Have each group member take one minute to ponder, then share, what they would do with one dollar, and with a thousand dollars.

61. Have each group member take one minute to describe their dream vacation.

62. Say I love you (or another common phrase) in 5-10 different languages, and allow group members to guess the origin/ native language for each one prior to saying the next one. These phrases are available on line.

63. Have group members announce what his or her new name would be if they could change their name, and why.

64. Sing "itsy bitsy spider" (or another popular children's song like popcorn popping on the apricot tree) together as a group. Make sure to use the hand motions too.

65. Everyone in group closes their eyes and while their eyes are closed, have them describe what the person next to them is wearing.

66. Each group member announces what a movie or book about their life would be titled.

67. Play word jumble with DBT skills: Have group members unravel the mixed letters to form the DBT skills. There are samples of word jumbles in part III of this book!

68. Pick any color and have each group member name an item or object that is likely to be that color.

69. Teach group members how to make an object using Origami.

70. Group members make a "new DBT skill" or anything else using the letters of their names as an acronym, with each letter representing a new word that describes them or something they enjoy doing.

71. Pass out small pieces of paper labeled with emotions or feelings and then have the group members act out the emotions or feelings in charade form for the other group members to guess. Helps members to observe and describe emotions.

72. Pass out colored pencils or crayons and then group members color one page out of a coloring book.

73. Bring a fishbowl to group with a goldfish or other colorful fish and observe the fish's fluid motions in the water. Group members describe their interpretation of the fish's movements.

74. Red Light Green Light: Group members form a single line, and a designated individual stands 20 feet away. Exercise leader has back to group, and then gives instructions for group members to go (advance towards leader) by stating "green light", and then group members stop advancing to group leader when group leader turns and faces them, saying "red light". Object is for group members to get close enough to leader to touch him or her, but group members cannot be caught moving during red light or when leader is facing them (only when back is turned).

75. Pass out pictures of animals and then have the group members construct a short story about the animal.

76. The Squeeze: Stand in circle, close eyes, and hold hands. Leader squeezes hand next to them. Then that member squeezes the hand of the other person next to

them. Send a pulse through the group. Do fast or slow.

77. Path: Create path between 2 people who have eyes closed. Make the distance approximately 5 feet. Third person walks between people and breaks an invisible barrier. If path makers sense person raise arms to block passage. This is similar to the game of playing "London Bridges Falling Down" but with your eyes closed. Be mindful of others' presence.

78. Tapping: Person taps areas of pressure points in gentle fashion with fleshy part of hand. This is a bodywork technique for staying grounded.

79. Kaleidoscope: Pass out small kaleidoscope toys for group members to look through for one minute.

80. Parachute: All group members hold sides of parachute and wave it up and down, feeling the sensation of rushing air and the power of air pressure. Rotate between fast and slow movements.

81. Laugh Exercise: Group continuous laughter (forced and spontaneous) for 2 minutes.

82. Blow large bubbles using bubble gum.

83. Blow liquid bubbles and pop them.

84. Hovering ping pong ball: Blow through straw with head tilted back, and watch the ping pong ball magically hover above the straw. May take a little practice.

85. Herb Delight: Bring in a variety of herbs like lavender, rosemary, thyme, cinnamon, etc. and with eyes closed have group members guess the herb that is placed under their nose.

86. Breathing Exercise: Have group members get comfortable in their chair, sitting upright with feet on the ground. Make sure their backs are straight as this makes it easier to breathe deeply. Try to have them keep their eyes open, gazing slightly downward. For the next three minutes, have group members focus on their breathing by counting as they breathe. Breathe in for the count of 3, hold your breath for a count of 2, breathe out for a count of 5, and hold for a count of 2. Repeat (in 3, hold 2, out 5, hold 2). As members notice their mind wandering or become aware

that they are distracted, have them notice the distraction, label it, and return their focus to the counting of their breath, starting again with an in-breath for 3 counts. Have group members begin and end with a signal or chime. A variation of this would be using popular words to breathe out, such as stress, tension, and negative energy. Popular words to breathe in are calm, serene, peace, etc.

87. Where's Waldo: Locate a large Where's Waldo book and play a few rounds of finding the goofy little character hidden in pictures.

88. Play a round of Sudoku.

89. Tic-Tac-Toe: Play a round or two of tic-tac-toe.

90. Complete a cross-word puzzle

91. Complete a word search exercise: Often found in the daily newspapers

92. Read the comics/ "funnies" section of a newspaper. Share with other group members.

93. Play a game of Jenga. Many other games that require skill and patience also work.

94. Complete a puzzle: Distribute small, mini puzzles to group members. Ask group members to be one mindfully in the moment with the puzzle. Encourage members to be aware of incoming thoughts or distracting thoughts, however work on letting go of the thought and refocusing on the puzzle. A variation of this is to have group members make their own puzzles.

95. Concentration: Gather a large tray with 20-30 small items (e.g., paper clip, piece of candy, battery, toy, thimble, button) scattered on it in single layer but not in obvious rows, paper and pencil for each participant. Keep the tray covered until just before the bell is rung. Instruct members as follows: "I have a tray full of items which I will uncover when I sound the bell. For the next three minutes, mindfully observe the items on the tray. Try to resist any urges to laugh, comment, or touch the items and continue to just observe. If your mind starts to wander or you get distracted, notice and label the distraction without judgment and bring your attention back to the items on the tray. I will end with the bell. After three

minutes, sound the bell and remove/cover the tray. Pass out paper and pencils. Ask members to spend the next minute making a list of everything they saw on the tray. Ask for feedback. (Did anyone include the tray? Were there some items everyone recalled seeing and others no one noticed?)

96. Write a poem or haiku: Allow group members an opportunity to share with other group members.

97. Pop Popcorn: Enjoy the popping sensation and natural or butter aroma.

98. Paper Airplane: Make a paper airplane or kite and fly them.

99. Rewrite a children's book: Find an old children's book with lots of colorful pictures and tear out each page. Shuffle the pages. Remove or cover page numbers, and have group members put the story back in order.

100. Long Word/Short Word: Write out on the board or tell the group members a very long word (i.e. "Personification"). Then give group members a specified amount of time to create new shorter words that can be made from the long word (i.e. person, son, cat, note, etc.).

101. Create your own mindfulness exercise or activity!

Part III: DBT Games & Activities

Dialectical Behavior Therapy (DBT) contains some very serious ideas, but it can also be a lot of fun to learn. This section has some great ideas for ways to help you learn the skills better. See if you are clever enough to complete some of our crossword puzzles filled with DBT words, or rearrange our jumbled DBT words. Or, perhaps you want to make your own Monopoly game with a DBT theme! We have included some helpful ways to make your DBT learning experience more interactive and just plain fun. In addition, this section has sample certificates for learning DBT and other general progress, and other helpful ideas for fun and interesting approaches to learning DBT. If you are planning on using this book with more than one person, you are more than welcome to photocopy the games in this section and then use those copies to write on or share with your friends that are also learning DBT! Note: These games are not part of the official DBT curriculum, but many of these activities contain DBT skills and themes and can be very helpful in assisting children, adolescents, and individuals of all ages remember the skills.

Across
4 not necessarily agreement
6 pleasant _____ to distract yourself
7 paying attention
9 jogging
11 logical ways to understand opposite ideas
13 truthful
14 use your lips to communicate
16 do you fall in _____ at first sight

Down
1 eat your favorite food
2 join the others
3 relationship help
5 watch what is happening
6 getting upset and reacting to others
8 the reason or purpose of it all
10 using five senses
11 explain the situation
12 cannot let these control us
15 give others a turn

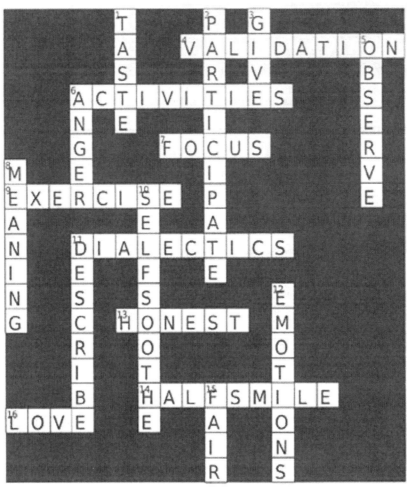

Across
4 not necessarily agreement
6 pleasant _____ to distract yourself
7 paying attention
9 jogging
11 logical ways to understand opposite ideas
13 truthful
14 use your lips to communicate
16 do you fall in _____ at first sight

Down
1 eat your favorite food
2 join the others
3 relationship help
5 watch what is happening
6 getting upset and reacting to others
8 the reason or purpose of it all
10 using five senses
11 explain the situation
12 cannot let these control us
15 give others a turn

Across

3 be honest
5 accept others without finding fault
8 just notice the experience
10 hold your moral ground
12 state your feelings about the situation
16 developed the whole DBT thing
17 when you are afraid

Down

1 bring yourself back to the moment
2 be an active member of group
3 things generated by your mind
4 sometimes call feelings
6 sometimes happens with remorse
7 taking care of your physical self
9 opposite of happiness
11 listen to some music
13 seeking wisdom from your higher power
14 eat some chocolate
15 equality for all involved

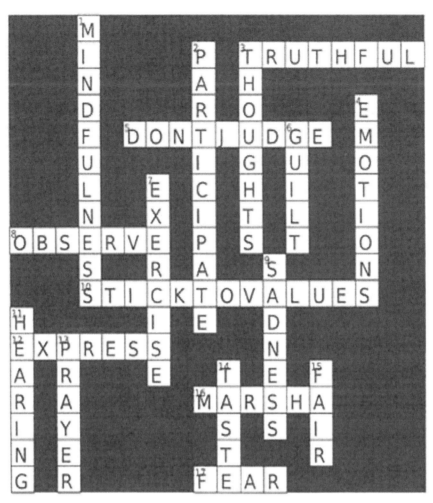

Across
3 be honest
5 accept others without finding fault
8 just notice the experience
10 hold your moral ground
12 state your feelings about the situation
16 developed the whole DBT thing
17 when you are afraid

Down
1 bring yourself back to the moment
2 be an active member of group
3 things generated by your mind
4 sometimes call feelings
6 sometimes happens with remorse
7 taking care of your physical self
9 opposite of happiness
11 listen to some music
13 seeking wisdom from your higher power
14 eat some chocolate
15 equality for all involved

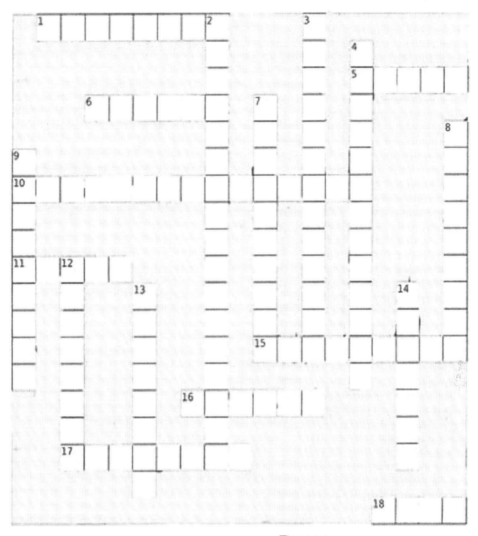

Across

1 put it into words
5 use a stress ball
6 be confident and ask for what you need
10 make eye contact and hold your ground
11 rest
15 barter, get what you need
16 look at a painting
17 must not control you
18 don't be distracted, take hold of this

Down

2 managing emotions
3 a healthy diet
4 distract yourself
7 process of helping others feel worthwhile
8 reward those who do right
9 your face reveals it all
12 consistent healthy activities to improve health
13 bring yourself to a higher place
14 imagine a perfect place you can go to

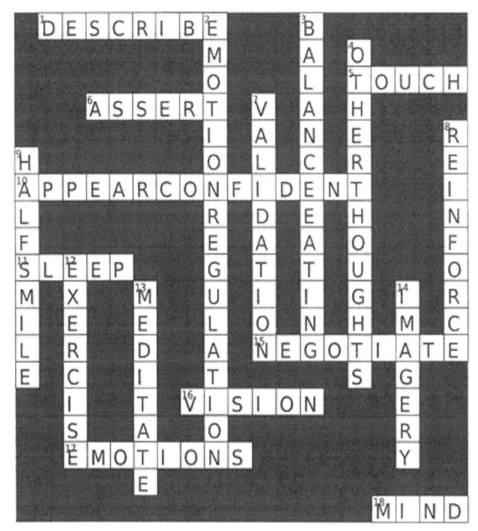

Across

1 put it into words
5 use a stress ball
6 be confident and ask for what you need
10 make eye contact and hold your ground
11 rest
15 barter, get what you need
16 look at a painting
17 must not control you
18 don't be distracted, take hold of this

Down

2 managing emotions
3 a healthy diet
4 distract yourself
7 process of helping others feel worthwhile
8 reward those who do right
9 your face reveals it all
12 consistent healthy activities to improve health
13 bring yourself to a higher place
14 imagine a perfect place you can go to

Across

1 a way to distract yourself
7 the type of therapy we do
8 ice in your hand
10 helping others feel real and worthwhile
11 keeping a relationship
12 be attentive and focused
16 coping with high levels of discomfort
17 making the moment better
18 effectively getting your needs met

Down

2 self statements of cheer
3 create a different emotion
4 stop fighting reality
5 maintaining self-respect
6 weighing the good and the bad
9 apply some lotion or eat some ice cream
13 eat, sleep, exercise, no drugs
14 what you experience with mood
15 not a full smile

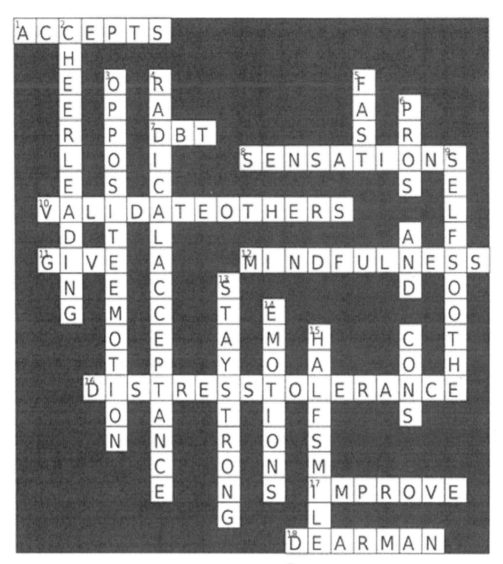

Across

1 a way to distract yourself
7 the type of therapy we do
8 ice in your hand
10 helping others feel real and worthwhile
11 keeping a relationship
12 be attentive and focused
16 coping with high levels of discomfort
17 making the moment better
18 effectively getting your needs met

Down

2 self statements of cheer
3 create a different emotion
4 stop fighting reality
5 maintaining self-respect
6 weighing the good and the bad
9 apply some lotion or eat some ice cream
13 eat, sleep, exercise, no drugs
14 what you experience with mood
15 not a full smile

Across

5 pet an animal
6 watch a movie, read a book, or count to 10
8 the opposite of sadness
11 look at a picture or watch for falling stars
12 light a scented candle
14 upturned lips with a relaxed face
16 cheer yourself on
17 cheerlead yourself
18 find or create a purpose in the pain

Down

1 become one with the moment or yourself
2 leave the situation for a while
3 imagine a relaxing scene
4 do something nice for someone else
7 read a funny book when you are sad
9 apply some lotion or eat some ice cream
10 breathe deep and let muscles unwind
13 taking time off
15 must be regulated

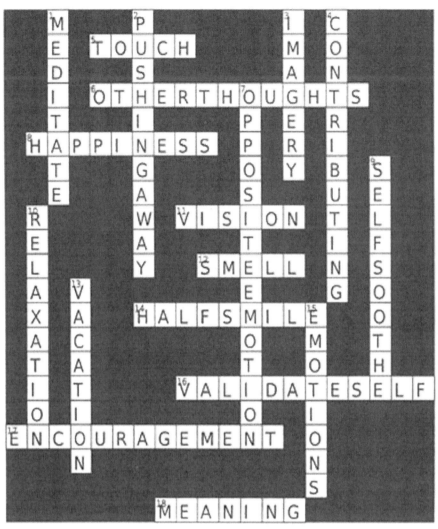

Across
5 pet an animal
6 watch a movie, read a book, or count to 10
8 the opposite of sadness
11 look at a picture or watch for falling stars
12 light a scented candle
14 upturned lips with a relaxed face
16 cheer yourself on
17 cheerlead yourself
18 find or create a purpose in the pain

Down
1 become one with the moment or yourself
2 leave the situation for a while
3 imagine a relaxing scene
4 do something nice for someone else
7 read a funny book when you are sad
9 apply some lotion or eat some ice cream
10 breathe deep and let muscles unwind
13 taking time off
15 must be regulated

h s m e f o m g k s n o i t o m e e
l e i t o l r a l s m h d i a n c l
o l d h e i e l e r e t i m t n l i
v f d b t t i s i e i a a p a s d m
s s l o i k a c e h e p l r n s c s
s o e s s g l s f t t e e o e c m f
d o p t o v n a t o a l c v e e g l
s t a s p n l i u e o d t e l o n a
i h t t p c o c r t n d i l s l i h
w e h u o w h i s a i i c l t p d o
o w d e g e d s s d e m s o a d a w
t s m n n o e o a i m h m g i v e s
l o c e i r r d c l v i g s k v l k
e c n a t p e c c a l a c i d a r i
m a r s c r a i i v a l i d a t e l
n o i t a l u g e r n o i t o m e l
l d n i m f o s e t a t s t i o h s
w i s e m i n d o f a s t p e c c a

dbt
halfsmile
middlepath
dialectics
prosandcons
accepts
statesofmind
improve
emotions
cheerleading
give
fast
smell
touch
taste
hearing
vision
validate
validateothers
validateself
howskills
whatskills
wisemind
middlepath
selfsoothe
radicalacceptance
distresstolerance
emotionregulation
actingopposite

e t i s o p p o g n i t c a d l o g n
c v a l i d a t e o t h e r s b t e n
n s s a e e w h m i d d l e p a t h c
a p t v a l i d a t e s e l f a s o s
t s r e t a s n c a i h p t d t a w r
p t i h o f e i c l r i a i p v i s a
e s t t s t m m e u t s l e i d u k a
c k n o a s i f p g t a c s l i t i e
c s n o u n n o t e v c i l p a w l h
a n i s c c d s s r a o e l l l m l u
l t i f n d h e i n n m i i h e i s t
a o a l h r n t g o s s l k c c d s t
c h e e r l e a d i n g i s t t d r g
I i c s d k d t s t v e e t i i l e h
d i s t r e s s t o l e r a n c e n s
a e v o r p m i e m r c w h s s p s l
r l s n o i t o m e c p e w t a a p e
g n i r a e h e e e h i d r i s t i a
w c l r d r t i e l i m s f l a h e i

cheerleading
vision
middlepath
dialectics
accepts
accepts
statesofmind
improve
emotions
dbt
give
prosandcons
distresstolerance
selfsoothe
taste
hearing
halfsmile
validate
validateothers
validateself
howskills
whatskills
actingopposite
middlepath
touch
radicalacceptance
smell
emotionregulation
wisemind

```
a s a c c e p t s e l f s o o t h e
s l l i k s t a h w r d i s h p c s
c o t v e g v a l i d a t e t n f s
i r a d i c a l a c c e p t a n c e
t i g v i s l l s c s h r r p s v n
c i e n e c i a d n s a e d e t a i
e h c u o t d o o s a l a n l p l p
l a e p d r a i n m o f s i d e i p
a m m e r n t s s t a s o m d c d a
i u o e r o e s s m l m n f i c a h
d l t c m l s s y t e i a o m a t s
s e i e o t e a s a e l b s i w e l
t e o g i r l a n o t e l e t e o n
s t n c t h f i d d s s e t s a t s
n u m s d t f a c i c o m a n i h l
n o i t a l u g e r n o i t o m e e
s d n u o s o o n i p g n s b c r s
m e d i t a t i o n n l d s t d s c
```

dialectics
vision
emotionregulation
cheerleading
accepts
statesofmind
accepts
emotions
dbt
fast
prosandcons
distresstolerance
halfsmile
taste
sounds
selfsoothe
validate
validateothers
validateself
whatskills
meditation
give
middlepath
touch
radicalacceptance
smell
happiness
reasonablemind
emotionmind

```
c a h l o a s c h o w s k i l l s
e c t a a h t a a h s r p t e l t
e c n a r e l o t s s e r t s i d
h e n c l f o a e t n h o h e c e
h p s a s m p n a i o t s e l h t
s t r m t e i y y c i o a a f e s
t s i o l p s r s k t e n d s e e
v l u d p t e l e t o t d n o r r
e c d a r g l c b o m a c i o l e
h i h o a e t d c v e d o m t e t
m e n m m a r s h a l i n e h a n
s g i s s e i o g l l l s s e d i
e b e t r u t h f u l a o i v i t
d t e c b e l t n e g v c w i n c
w h a t s k i l l s l o s i g g a
n i a s t a t e s o f m i n d d v
d s l n s d n u o s t p e c c a r
o d h i o o t n o i t a x a l e r
```

wisemind
relaxation
marshalinehan
cheerleading
accepts
statesofmind
accepts
emotions
dbt
middlepath
prosandcons
distresstolerance
halfsmile
taste
sounds
selfsoothe
sticktovalues
validateothers
betruthful
howskills
gentle
whatskills
give
touch
radicalacceptance
smell
happiness
imagery
actinterested

```
t e o y g a v d l m a r d e g o s i
e s p c c n o i t a x a l e r d r s
i e p y h s i m a g e r y v b n b a
d l o t h e r t h o u g h t s o m c
n f s p n n e w u c c o m b h s a c
a s i d p m o r a b e x e r c i s e
h o t n s o p d l n i t o b s r t p
a o e i p e s h r e r r t c p a e t
l t e m c u i i t u a l t r e p r s
f h m f x k s t t a g d o n h m y a
s e o o t r h i e p s i m o o a f
m e t s a t f o i v a e a n f c t p
i n i e l u o r v n i c l s g t l u
l e o t l e s u d a g t t d y i a d
e c n a t p e c c a l a c i d a r e
h e s t n p o p r h i u w a o i l u
e n s s e n i p p a h s e a a n m n
t e a o s e n s a t i o n s y e m x
```

Oppositeaction
relaxation
sensations
cheerleading
oppositeemotion
accepts
statesofmind
sleep
mastery
dbt
middlepath
prosandcons
comparison
halfsmile
taste
pushing away
selfsoothe
sticktovalues
eat
betruthful
otherthoughts
activities
exercise
fast
touch
radicalacceptance
nodrugs
happiness
imagery
contributing

DBT House:
(Give these instructions to your client) You are going to create your own house. Draw an outline of your house and make your house 4 levels. Along the foundation of the house, write the values that govern your life. Along the walls write anything or anyone that supports you. On the roof, write the things that protect you. On the door write the things that you keep hidden from others. In the chimney, write ways that you blow off steam. On the billboard, write the things that you are proud of and what you want others to see.

Within the levels of your house, describe how you feel at each level and explain what it takes for you to reach the top of your house (to be at your best!!!). In level one (the basement) you are going to list all the behaviors that you are trying to gain control of in your life. In level two you are going to list/draw all the emotions that you are attempting to experience more fully and in a healthier way. In level three you are going to list all the things in your life you would like to be happy about or are happy about. In level four you are going to talk about or draw what a "Life Worth Living" would look like for you. Here are the levels:

Level 1: Behavior Dyscontrol (external)   **Behavior Control**
Level 2: Quiet Desperation (internal)   **Emotional Experiencing**
Level 3: Problems in Living (school problems) **Ordinary**
                                               Happiness/Unhappiness
Level 4: Incompleteness (lonely, empty)   **Capacity for Joy & Freedom**

DBT Charms:
Purchase several charm bracelets and a variety of charms. Designate certain charms for each module (example: a heart charm could represent emotion regulation). Individuals earn the charms for learning each skill module. Have individuals discuss what the goal(s) of the module are, specific skills within each module, what the acronyms mean, how they have used the skill, etc. Once you feel they have adequately demonstrated successful understanding of the skill present them the skills charm during skills group. During a session individuals can test out one-on-one or in a group setting. Have individuals earn charms for other individual successes.

Self-Soothe Kit:
Have your client identify for each of the 5 senses activities or things that are soothing to them. Then assist them in developing a self-soothe kit to carry with them and use as needed to tolerate distressing situations. This can be done in a residential setting as a behavioral modification program; having the residents earning components of their self-soothe kit. At home parents can support their children in earning components of their self-soothe kit by completing various tasks or demonstrating effective skill use. Make it fun!

DBT Charades:
Write out specific DBT skills or components of the DBT skills on separate pieces of paper. Then place in a container for members to draw skills from. Have members act out, following the typical rules of charades (no talking, no sounds, etc.), what is on the piece of paper while the other participants attempt to guess the DBT skill or components of the skills. Variation: Emotion charades, write out specific emotions, and then have members act out the emotion picked from the container while the other members attempt to guess the emotion. This variation can allow for discussion about how emotions are communicated non-verbally and can assist with the development of the components of core mindfulness observing and describing.

DBT Jeopardy:
Develop several clues about each of the DBT skills and/or specific components. The categories can be the 5 modules: core mindfulness, walking the middle path, distress tolerance, emotion regulation and interpersonal effectiveness. Develop different questions of varying levels of difficulty for each category. Then divide the group members into teams or play individually; the object of the team or individual is to guess the skill or component of the skill that the clue is describing (example clue: "This skill assists with developing new relationships or maintaining current relationships." Answer: "What is GIVE?"). This allows group members to learn the DBT skills in a fun way!

A DBT Play:
Develop as a group a "DBT Play" that incorporates as many examples (positive and negative) of DBT skills into the play storyline that the group can include. After the play have the group process the positive examples of DBT skill demonstration and the times within the play when DBT skills could have been used.

DBT Infomercials:
Have group members break into smaller groups (2-3 members in each group) and have them pick a skill that they really like. Next discuss with the group what an infomercial is and the components of an infomercial (example: product (skill), special offer, why buy product (skill), what makes product (skill) so good, what number to call, etc.). Then have each small group create an infomercial selling their skill including all the important components agreed on as a large group. Present the infomercials to the large group.

DBT Cheers:
Write up a cheer that you can remember for yourself that can be used when you are struggling, falling into an interpersonal myth, dealing with a factor that is reducing your interpersonal effectiveness, etc. Share with your therapist or with the group.

DBT Collage:
Make a collage of your favorite skill and how you remember the skills (example: Engaging in Pleasant Activities collage with all the pleasant activities you like to do).

Personalized DBT License Plate:
Create a personalized license plate to hang on your wall, door, locker, etc. that includes one or all of your favorite DBT skills to assist with skill integration and generalization.

Visualization of the States of Mind:
Create the circles of emotion mind, reasonable mind, and wise mind. Color each of the states of mind the way they are visually represented in your mind. Share the meaning of the coloring with your therapist or the skills group.

Media DBT:
Bring in a variety of different pre-selected movie clips. Have the group members view the various movie clips and identify effective use of DBT skills, ineffective use of DBT skills and times when DBT skills could have been used to better regulate the situation/emotion.

Mural of DBT:

Use a large mural size piece of paper; tape it to a smooth wall; create a topic that will be the focus of the mural (example: ways to self-soothe); then have members take turns writing/drawing what they think about the topic of the mural and/or answering the topic question of the mural. Keep up as a reminder of skills, as inspiration to use the skills, or as a variety of suggestions for different ways to use the skill.

DBT Life Worth Living Collage:

Make a collage of all the factors that contribute to creating a life worth living and process with your therapist or the group.

DBT Flower of Emotions:

Use a large piece of paper and have your client draw a flower with petals; then have them list all the emotions they experience in each of the petals; next have them write in each petal how they have been coping with and tolerating each emotion up to this point. After that, on the other side of the paper have them draw a flower again with petals and list all their emotions; then have them list all the DBT skills and healthy ways they can experience a continuum of emotions.

DBT MONOPOLY

To make your DBT Monopoly game, you will need an original or variation of any Monopoly version, because you will be using some of that game's items. You must substitute our new instructions that have been modified for DBT skill acquisition and application. It can be a really fun project for a small or large group of people. Just photocopy the instructions that are included later in this book, and cut out the new game pieces to make your own DBT Monopoly playing board. If you have an original board, paper money, dice, houses, and player tokens, all the rest of the pieces are here for you to copy and use. You just need a large posterboard or other piece of paper to paste the game pieces to, or you can simply cut the cards to the size of the original playing board property sizes and just paste the pieces to the board. Instructions start on the following page! Following the instructions, you will find the individual property pieces, a new center logo (on this page), and even the chance and community chest card content which you can modify or personalize as you see fit, and then put each of those statements on cards of the appropriate color using regular construction paper. You will be substituting some new properties for some of the old Monopoly properties. You can use the regular title deed cards if you color the blank squares in this book for each skill to match the cards from your existing monopoly game. In addition, you can now call the green plastic house pieces treatment centers. You can call the red plastic hotel pieces hospitals. The utilities and railroads can stay the same. Since this will be your game and your project, feel free to make other modifications as you see appropriate for your learning experience. Be creative, and have fun learning DBT!

DBT MONOPOLY
The Fun Skill Ownership Game
Ages 8 to Adult, 2 to 8 Players

In the early 1990's, Marsha Linehan incorporated aspects of many treatment approaches to develop a new treatment called Dialectical Behavior Therapy (DBT). For the most part, DBT combined cognitive and behavioral treatments with Eastern meditation and mindfulness practices. This therapy has proven very helpful for individuals with Borderline Personality Disorder or similar traits worldwide. In addition, countless other people have found DBT skills helpful for daily stress management and emotional regulation.

One day a handful of clinicians realized that their patients enjoyed playing all kinds of games. They saw this as an opportunity to make learning DBT skills even more fun! DBT Monopoly combines the useful skills of Dialectical Behavior Therapy with the ever-popular game of Monopoly!

Object: The object of the game is to own the most DBT skill properties through reviewing, learning, applying, buying, renting, and selling skills (skill properties).

Equipment: The equipment consists of the DBT skill properties and content found in this book, and the regular pieces included with the original game such as a board, 2 dice, tokens, 32 treatment centers (green), and 12 hospitals (red), play money, and a Banker's tray. You can use the existing player pieces or choose any other marker or toy to move around the board. After all, it is your game!

Preparation: Photocopy the skill property pieces from the following pages. Then, color and cut out the individual pieces that you have just photocopied. Arrange and paste the new pieces in place of the old properties, using the colors and property prices as your guide for which colors each new skill property should have. The new skill properties have prices that match up with the correct original Monopoly property place, so it will be easier for you to know where each piece should go. Place the board on a table and put your newly designed DBT Chance and Community Chest cards face down on their allotted spaces on the board. Each player chooses a token to represent him/her while traveling around the board. Each player is given $1500 divided as follows: 2 each of $500s, $100s and $50s; 6 $20s; 5 each of $10s, $5s, and $1s. All remaining money and other equipment go to the Bank. Stack the Bank's money on the edge in the compartments in the plastic Banker's tray.

Banker: Select as Banker a player who will also make a good judge and auctioneer. A Banker who plays in the games must keep his/her personal funds separate from those of the Bank. When more than five persons play, the Banker may elect to act only as Banker and Auctioneer. The Banker also has the important role of making sure other players read aloud the skill summaries prior to buying, selling, and mortgaging skill properties. (See DBT advanced play for additional roles assumed by the Banker).

The Bank: Besides the Bank's money, the Bank holds the Title Deed cards for each skill property (the property deed cards are the original cards that match up with the new card color and price, or you can make your own DBT skill property deed cards), and treatment centers and hospitals prior to purchase and use by the players. The Bank pays salaries and bonuses. It sells and auctions skill properties and hands out their proper Title Deed cards. It sells treatment centers and hospitals to the players and loans money when required on mortgages. The Bank collects all taxes, fines, loans and interest, and the price of all skill properties, which it sells and auctions. The Bank never goes broke. If the Bank runs out of money, the Banker may issue as much more as may be needed by writing on any ordinary paper.

The Play: Starting with the Banker, each player in turn throws the dice. The player with the highest total starts the play. Place your token on the corner marked GO, throw the dice and move your token in the direction the arrow the number of spaces indicated by the dice. After you have completed your play, the turn passes to the left. The tokens remain on the spaces occupied and proceed from that point on the player's next turn. Two or more tokens may rest on the same space at the same time. According to the space your token reaches, you may be entitled to buy skill property or other properties, or you may be obliged to pay for "treatment" if you land on someone else's skill property and they have treatment centers or hospitals. You may have to pay various other treatment fees, draw a DBT Chance or Community Chest card, or you may have to go straight to the main Hospital! If you throw doubles, you move your token as usual, the sum of two dice, and are subject to the privileges or penalties pertaining to the space on which you land. Retaining the dice, throw again and move your token as before. If you throw doubles three times in succession, move your token immediately to the main Hospital (see Hospital).

GO: Each time a player's token lands on or passes over GO, whether by throwing the dice or drawing a card, the Banker pays him/her a $200 salary. The $200 is paid only once each time around the board. However, if a player passing GO on the throw of the dice lands 2 spaces beyond it on a Community Chest, or 7 spaces beyond it on a DBT Chance, and draws the Advance to GO card, he/she collects $200 for passing GO the first time and another $200 for reaching it the second time by instructions on the card.

Buying Skill Property: Whenever you land on an unowned skill property or other unowned property you may buy that property from the Bank at its printed price. However, before doing so, you must read aloud the skill summary as listed on the back of the Title Deed card for that property. You then own the skill property. Place that card face up in front of you. If you do not wish to buy property, the Banker sells it at auction to the highest bidder. The buyer pays the Bank the amount of the bid in cash and receives the Title Deed card for that property. Any player, except for the one who declined the option to buy it at the printed price, may bid. Bidding may start at any price. If another player wants to purchase land being auctioned, they must read aloud the skill named for that property after the auction is won, but before that player is given the Title Deed card.

Paying for Treatment: When you land on a skill property or other property owned by another player, the owner collects treatment payment from you in accordance with the fees printed on its Title Deed card. If the property is mortgaged, no fees can be collected. When a property is mortgaged, its Title Deed card is placed face down in front of the owner. It is an advantage to hold all the Title Deed cards in a color group (e.g., Accepts and Self-Soothe; or States of Mind, Mindfulness What Skills, and Mindfulness How Skills) because the owner may then charge double fees for unimproved skill properties in that color-group. This rule applies to unmortgaged properties even if another property in that color group is mortgaged. It is even more advantageous to have treatment centers or hospitals on skill properties because fees are much higher than for unimproved properties. The owner may not collect the fees if he/she fails to before the second player following throws the dice.

DBT Chance and Community Chest: When you land on either of these spaces, take the top card from the deck indicated, follow the instructions and return the card face down to the bottom of the deck. The Get Out of Hospital Free card is held until used and then returned to the bottom of the deck. If the player who draws it does not wish to use it, he/she may sell it, at any time, to another player at a price agreeable to both.

Hospital (Main): You land in the Hospital when…(1) your token lands on the space marked "Go to Hospital"; (2) you draw a card marked "Go to Hospital"; or (3) you throw doubles three times in succession. When you are sent to the Hospital (main Hospital, not little hospitals on players' properties) you cannot collect $200 salary in that move since, regardless of where your token is on the board, you must move it directly to the Hospital. Your turn ends when you are sent to the Hospital. If you are not "sent" to the Hospital, but in the ordinary course of play land on that space, you are "Just Visiting," you incur no penalty, and you move ahead in the usual manner on your next turn. You get out of the Hospital by… (1) throwing doubles on any of your next three turns; if you succeed in doing this you immediately move forward the number of spaces shown by your doubles throw; even though you had thrown doubles, you do not take another turn; (2) using the "Get Out of Hospital Free" card if you have it; (3) purchasing the "Get Out of Hospital Free" card from another player; (4) paying a fee of $50 before you roll the dice on either of your next two turns; (5) correctly identifying and summarizing any three DBT skills (also listed at the end of these instructions). If you do not throw doubles by your third turn, or if you are unable to correctly identify and summarize three skills as determined by the judge, you must pay the $50 fine. You then get out of the Hospital and immediately move forward the number of spaces shown by your throw. Even though you are in the Hospital, you may buy and sell skill property, buy and sell treatment centers and hospitals, and collect skill property fees.

Free Parking: A player landing on this space does not receive any money, property or reward of any kind. This is just a "free" resting place.

Treatment Centers (green): When you own all the skill properties in a color group you may buy treatment centers from the Bank and erect them on those properties. If you buy one treatment center, you may put it on any one of those skill properties. However, for each treatment center or hospital you purchase for your property, you must first re-read aloud the skill named for that property. The next treatment center you buy must be erected on one of the other unimproved skill properties of this or any other complete color skill property group you may own. The price you must pay the bank for each treatment center is shown on your Title Deed card for the skill property on which you erect the treatment center. The owner still collects double fees from an opponent who lands on the unimproved properties of his/her complete color-group. Following the above rules, you may buy and erect at any time treatment centers as your judgment and financial standing will allow. But you must build evenly, i.e., you cannot erect more than one treatment center on any one skill property of any color-group until you have built one treatment center on every skill property of that group. You may then begin on the second row of treatment centers, and so on, up to a limit of four treatment centers to a skill property. For example, you cannot build three treatment centers for one skill property if you have only one treatment center on another skill property of that same color-group. Again, before you purchase any new treatment center, you must first read aloud the skill for which that property was named. As you build evenly, you must also break down evenly if you sell skill properties back to the Bank (see Selling Property).

Hospitals (red): When a player has four treatment centers on each skill property within a complete color-group, he/she may buy a Hospital from the bank and erect it on any property of the color-group. He/she returns the four treatment centers from that skill property to the Bank and pays the price for the Hospital as shown on the Title Deed card. Only one Hospital may be erected on any one skill property. Before you purchase any new Hospital, you must first read aloud the skill for which that property was named.

Buying Shortages: When the Bank has no treatment centers to sell, players wishing to build must wait for some player to return or sell his/her treatment centers to the Bank before building. If there are a limited number of treatment centers and Hospitals available and two or more players wish to buy more than the Bank has, the treatment centers or Hospitals must be sold at auction to the highest bidder. Again, before a player can buy any skill property, treatment center, or Hospital, he/she must first read aloud the skill named for that property.

Selling Property: Unimproved properties and utilities (but not buildings) may be sold to any player as a private transaction for any amount the owner can get; however, no property can be sold to another player if buildings are standing on any properties of that color-group. Any buildings so located must be sold back to the Bank before the owner can sell any skill property of that color-group. Treatment centers and Hospitals may be sold back to the Bank at any time for one-half the price paid for them. All treatment centers on one color-group must be sold one by one, evenly, in reverse of the manner in which they were erected. All Hospitals on one color-group may be sold at once, or they may be sold one treatment center at a time (one Hospital equals five treatment centers), evenly, in reverse of the manner in which they were erected.

Mortgages: Unimproved skill properties can be mortgaged through the Bank at any time. Before an improved skill property can be mortgaged, all the buildings on all the properties of its color-group must be sold back to the Bank at half price. The mortgage value is printed on each Title Deed card. No fees for players landing on your property can be collected on mortgaged skill properties or utilities, but fees can be collected on unmortgaged skill properties in the same group. In order the lift the mortgage, the owner must pay the Bank the amount of the mortgage plus 10% interest. When all the skill properties of a color-group are no longer mortgaged, the owner may begin to buy back treatment centers at full price. The player who mortgages property retains possession of it and not other player may secure it by lifting the mortgage from the Bank. However, the owner may sell this mortgaged property to another player at any agreed price. If you are the new owner, you may lift the mortgage at once if you wish by paying off the mortgage plus 10%. If the mortgage is not lifted at once, you must pay the Bank 10% interest when you buy the skill property and if you lift the mortgage later you must pay the bank an additional 10% interest as well as the amount of the mortgage.

Bankruptcy: You are declared bankrupt if you owe more than you can pay either to another player or to the Bank. If your debt is to another player, you must turn over to that player all that you have of value and retire from the game. However, that player cannot accept any of your properties without first reading aloud the skills for which each of the properties are named. If you own treatment centers or Hospitals, you must return these to the Bank in exchange for money to the extent of one-half the amount paid for them; this cash is given to the creditor. If you have mortgaged property you also turn that over to your creditor but the new owner must at once pay the Bank the amount of interest on the loan, which is 10% of the value of the property. Should you owe the bank, instead of another player, more than you can pay (because of fees or penalties), even by selling off buildings and mortgaging property, you must turn over all assets to the Bank. In this case, the Bank immediately sells by auction all property so taken, except buildings. Skills for which properties were named must be read aloud prior to new purchase. A bankrupt player must immediately retire from the game. The last player left in the game wins!

Miscellaneous: Money can be loaned to another player only by the Bank and then only by mortgaging property. No player may borrow or lend money to another player.

Advanced Play: All rules of regular DBT Monopoly apply, but players are required to summarize from memory (not just read aloud) the skills named for each property prior to all transactions. The Banker acts as Judge to determine if at least 75% of the skill has been summarized by the player. This game is recommended strictly for use with a DBT skill leader to serve as Banker and Judge. The skills can be summarized as those included at the end of these instructions or summarized as those included in Part 1 of this book.

Rules for Short Game (60 to 90 minutes): There are five changed rules for this first Short Game.

1. During Preparation (see Preparation if needed), the Banker shuffles then deals three Title Deed cards to each player. These are free-no payment to the Bank is required.
2. You need only three treatment centers (instead of four) on each lot of a complete color-group before you can by a Hospital. Hospital fees remain the same. The turn-in value is still one-half the purchase price, which in this game is one treatment center less than in the regular game.
3. If you land in the Hospital, you must exit on your next turn by (1) using a "Get Out of Hospital Free" card if you have (or can buy) one; or (2) rolling doubles; or (3) paying $50; or (4) immediately summarize three DBT skills among those listed within these instructions. Unlike the standard rules, you may try to roll doubles and, failing to do so, pay the $50 on the same turn.
4. The penalty for landing on "Income Tax" is a flat $200.
5. End of Game: The game ends when one player goes bankrupt. The remaining players value their property: (1) cash on hand; (2) lots, utilities, and other properties owned; (3) any mortgaged property owned, at one-half the price printed on the board; (4) treatment centers, valued at purchase price; (5) Hospitals, valued at purchase price including the value of the three treatment centers turned in. All rules of reading aloud skills prior to purchase of each property still apply.

The richest (most skilled) player wins!

Time Limit Game: Before starting, agree upon a definite hour of termination, when the richest player will be declared the winner. Before starting, the Banker shuffles and cuts the Title Deed cards and deals two to each player. Players immediately pay the Bank the price of the properties dealt to them. Reading skill summaries aloud are still required, or the player forfeits the properties back to the Bank.

Here are the skills each player must read before buying or selling property.

DIALECTICAL BEHAVIORAL THERAPY (DBT) SKILLS[3]

INTERPERSONAL EFFECTIVENESS SKILLS:

Cheerleading Statements: Statements people make to themselves in order to give themselves permission to ask for what they need or want, to say no, and to act effectively. These statements provide the courage to act, help in preparing for a situation, and counteract myths about interpersonal behavior.

DEAR MAN: This skill assists individuals with getting their objectives met by using effective means of being clear, concise, and assertive.

Describe-Describe the situation & stick to the facts.

Express-Express your feelings about the situation; use "I feel" statements.

Assert-Assert yourself by asking for what you want or saying no clearly; remember others cannot read your mind.

Reinforce-Reinforce the other person ahead of time by explaining the positive effects of getting what you want; reward the person afterwards.

Mindfully-Take hold of your mind; keep your focus on what you want; don't be distracted.

Appear Confident-Use a confident tone of voice; make good eye contact.

Negotiate-Be willing to give to get; offer other solutions.

GIVE: This skill assists individuals in developing, maintaining, or ending relationships to maintain healthy relationships in one's life.

(be) **G**entle-Be nice and respectful; no attacks, no threats; no judging; notice your voice tone.

(act) **I**nterested-Listen to the other person; don't interrupt; be patient; make eye contact; don't make faces.

Validate-Show you understand the other person's feelings and situation.

(use an) **E**asy Manner-Use a little humor and smile; use non-threatening body language.

FAST: This skill assists individuals in gaining mastery and self-respect through sticking to one's values and beliefs; being fair and honest.

(be) **F**air-Be fair to yourself and to the other person.

(no) **A**pologies-Don't over apologize.

Stick to Values-Stick to your own values.

(be) **T**ruthful-Don't lie; don't act helpless when you are not.

DISTRESS TOLERANCE SKILLS:

SELF-SOOTHE: This skill assists individuals in learning to use their five senses to comfort, nurture, be gentle, and be kind to manage distressing situations effectively.

- Vision, Hearing, Smell, Taste, & Touch.

ACCEPTS: This skill assists individuals in learning how to practice distracting interventions when distressing events occur to manage distress effectively.

Activities-Call or visit a friend, go to a movie, play a sport, etc.

Contributing-Give something to someone, do something nice for someone.

Comparison-Compare yourself to others coping with situations, remind yourself of all the good things in your life.

With Opposite **E**motion-Read an emotional book or story, listen to emotional music, be sure the event creates different emotions than what you are currently feeling.

Pushing Away-Push the situation away by leaving it for awhile; build an imaginary wall between yourself and the situation.

With Other **T**houghts-Count colors in a picture, work on a crossword puzzle, watch TV, etc.

With Intense Other **S**ensations-Hold ice in your hand, take a very hot or very cold shower, squeeze a rubber ball.

IMPROVE: This skill assists individual in using methods to improve the current moment with positive events.

Imagery-Create a different situation in your mind, day dream, imagine coping with a situation.

Meaning-Focus on the positives of a painful situation, make lemonade out of lemons.

Prayer-This is the complete opening of oneself to the moment; using one's spirituality.

Relaxation-Change how the body responds to stress, listen to relaxing music, use deep breathing strategies.

One thing in the Moment-Focus your attention and increase your awareness to the moment; put your mind in the present moment; do awareness exercises.

Take a **V**acation-Go on a brief retreat from coping or actively managing the current situation; allow oneself to be taken care of for the moment.

Encouragement-Cheerlead oneself through the moment.

Pros & Cons: Think about the positive and negative aspects of tolerating distress and the positive and negative aspects of not tolerating the distress. Focus on long term goals; think of the positive consequences of tolerating the distress.

Half-Smile: Accept reality with your face; a half-smile is slightly up-turned lips with a relaxed face.

Radical Acceptance: Let go of fighting reality when you cannot keep painful events, emotions, and life circumstances from coming your way. Accept from deep within yourself what is and just as it is by entering into reality, just as it is, at this moment. Remember radical acceptance is not approval, passivity, or against change.

Turning the Mind: Choosing to accept and make an inner commitment to accept; this commitment is the first step toward acceptance. You have to turn your mind and commit to acceptance over and over and over again.

Willingness: Accepting what is, together with responding to what is, in an effective or appropriate manner. Do what works and do just what is needed in the current moment.

EMOTION REGULATION SKILLS & BUILD DAILY STRENGTH:

Build Daily Strength*: Practicing healthy habits of daily living each day helps keep people emotionally regulated. Exercising, taking care of your body, eating right, not using illegal drugs or alcohol, sleeping well, and building self mastery (doing fun activities and things that we enjoy) into daily practice.

Balance Sleep: Practice healthy sleep habits; Take Care of Self: Take care of your body; Resist Target Behaviors: Avoid harmful activities; Get Exercise: Exercise daily; Balance Nutrition: Eat foods that are good for you; Gain Mastery: Take charge once a day; Take Time for Yourself: Do something fun daily; Healthy Self-Talk: Say nice things about yourself.

OPPOSITE ACTION: Change current emotion by acting opposite to the current emotional urge. (Example: Feeling sadness leads to the urge of isolation or avoidance; get active, approach, do things that make you feel competent.)

Mindfulness of Current Emotions: Let go of emotional suffering by experiencing your emotion as it occurs, practice mindfulness of emotional body sensations, remind yourself you are not your emotion, and practice loving your emotion.

CORE MINDFULNESS SKILLS:

STATES OF MIND: This skill assists individuals in learning to be in control of their own mind, instead of letting the mind be in control of them. The three states of mind are emotion mind, reasonable mind, and wise mind. Reasonable mind is the rational, thinking, logical mind. Emotion mind is when your emotions are in control of your thinking and your behavior. Wise mind is the integration of emotion mind and reasonable mind. The ultimate goal is to integrate one's emotion mind and reasonable mind; hence achieving wise mind.

WHAT Skills: These skills assist individuals in practicing "what to do" to engage in the core mindfulness skills effectively. The WHAT skills include *observe* (just notice the experience), *describe* (use words to represent what you observed), and *participate* (become one with your experience).

HOW Skills: These skills assist individuals in practicing "how to" engage in the core mindfulness skills effectively. The HOW skills include *be nonjudgmental* (see but don't evaluate the experience), *one-mindfully* (stay focused, do one thing at a time), and *effectively* (do what works; focus on the things that work).

WALKING THE MIDDLE PATH SKILLS:

VALIDATE SELF & VALIDATE OTHERS: Quietly reassure yourself that what you feel is real, important, and makes sense. Validate others by observing the experience and describing non-judgmentally the facts, the person's inherent worth, the unstated feelings, and/or what is valid about the person's experience.

DIALECTICS: It teaches individuals that there is more than one true way to see a situation and more than one way to solve a problem. In addition, dialectics stresses the importance of not looking at the world in absolutes, rather looking at the world in terms of both/and or finding the middle path between acceptance and change.

*non DBT skill, but similar to many DBT skills.

Use our ideas for DBT Community Chest cards or make your own cards (Yellow)!

Validate each player: Collect $50 from each player you validate on this turn

Purchase self-soothe kits: $40 per treatment center, $115 for Hospital

You used your Wise Mind: Collect $50

You made a skills coaching call: Pay $50

Psychiatrists Fee: $50

Explain Radical Acceptance: Collect $100

Get out of Hospital Free: This card may be kept until needed or sold to a peer

Pay Hospital $100

At risk behavior: Go straight to Main Hospital, Do not Pass Go, Do not Collect $200!

Additional therapy session for relationship stress: Pay $50

Early Discharge from treatment: Collect $100

Go to Hospital. Go directly to hospital! Do not pass go. Do Not Collect $200

Therapist Error in Your Favor: Collect $200

Pay Therapy Fees: Pay $150

You have been engaging in positive Self-Validation: Collect $50

Your Interpersonal Effective Skills Pay Off: Collect $100

Use our ideas for DBT Chance cards, or make your own cards (Orange)!

Describe a time when you didn't use a skill and what you could have used to be more effective: PAY $50

Identify and describe one skill used today: COLLECT $50

Observe and describe current emotion, then Advance to Go and Collect $200

Advance to Self-Soothe Avenue

You are able to help a peer learn new skills today: Collect $100

You need the assistance of a friend to identify a skill: Pay $100

Make general repairs on all your skill properties: For each treatment center pay $25 and for each Hospital pay $100

This card may be kept until needed or sold: Get Out of Hospital Free!

Soothe yourself: Advance to Self-Soothe skill property.

Advance to Half-Smile: If you pass go, collect $200

Go directly to hospital: Do not pass go, do not collect $200

You have been found to invalidate others: Pay each player $50

THINK AND ACT
DIALECTICAL
PRICE: $60

VALIDATE SELF
AND OTHERS
PRICE: $60

STATES OF
MIND
PRICE: $100

MINDFULNESS
WHAT SKILLS

PRICE: $100

MINDFULNESS
HOW SKILLS

PRICE: $120

MINDFULNESS
OF CURRENT
EMOTIONS
PRICE: $140

OPPOSITE
ACTION
PRICE: $140

BUILD DAILY
STRENGTH
PRICE: $160

BALANCE
SLEEP
PRICE: $180

TAKE CARE
OF SELF
PRICE: $180

RESIST TARGET
BEHAVIORS
PRICE: $200

DEAR MAN
PRICE: $220

GIVE AND FAST

PRICE: $220

CHEERLEADING
STATEMENTS
PRICE: $240

WILLINGNESS

PRICE: $260

TURNING
THE MIND
PRICE: $260

HALF SMILE

PRICE: $280

PROS AND CONS

PRICE: $300

IMPROVE

PRICE: $300

RADICAL
ACCEPTANCE

PRICE: $320

ACCEPTS

PRICE: $350

SELF SOOTHE

Price $400

Hospital

Go To

Just Visiting

Hospital!

Appendix A

Here are some pages for you to color. Coloring can be very relaxing and mindful. We think it is better to photocopy these pages and then color on the copies. That way, you can share with your friends and color the DBT skills more than once, and as many different ways as you want. Enjoy!

MIDDLE PATH

INTERPERSONAL EFFECTIVENESS

DBT EMOTION
FLOWER

MY DBT HOUSE

DISTRACT WITH A<u>C</u>CEPTS USING CONTRIBUTING

IMPROVE THE MOMENT WITH IMAGERY

Remember PROS & CONS

THINK & ACT DIALECTICALLY

Remember people can have different points of view when looking at a situation!!!!!!

Cheerleading Statements

Self-Soothe With
The 5 Senses

YOUR DBT HOUSE

Improve the Moment
with Relaxation

ENGAGE IN A PLEASANT ACTIVITY

Half-Smile

Consider the Pros and Cons

WALK THE MIDDLE PATH

Build and Keep Relationships
With GIVE and FAST

Appendix B

This is a cool cash coupon that can be traded in for candy, rewards, privileges, or whatever else you work out with your DBT skill trainers or parents.

CONGRATULATIONS! This coupon means you have earned

COOL CASH

_____

_____

_____

_____

Earning a COOL CASH COUPON means you have done a
wonderful job and deserve a special reward!!! We are proud
of you and your hard work!!!

_____

Signature

_____

Date

Appendix C

This is a certification of skill group completion or participation. Add your own stickers or bright colors!

DBT PARTICIPATATION AWARD

This award goes to: _____ for your remarkable participation in DBT skills group. You should be proud of all your hard work and dedication. You have developed and demonstrated some amazing skill growth!!!!! We are proud of you!!!

Signed: _____   Date: _____

Appendix D

This is a skills card for monitoring skill use. Also included is a diary card for monitoring behaviors and emotions.

Dialectical Behavior Therapy – Adolescent Skills Card

Instructions: Mark the days you worked on each skill.

#	Skill	M	T	W	TH	F	S	S	#	Skill	M	T	W	TH	F	S	S
1.	Wise Mind	M	T	W	TH	F	S	S	15.	Engaging in pleasant activities	M	T	W	TH	F	S	S
2.	Observe	M	T	W	TH	F	S	S	16.	Working toward long-term goals	M	T	W	TH	F	S	S
3.	Describe	M	T	W	TH	F	S	S	17.	IMPROVE	M	T	W	TH	F	S	S
4.	Participate	M	T	W	TH	F	S	S	18.	ACCEPTS	M	T	W	TH	F	S	S
5.	Don't Judge	M	T	W	TH	F	S	S	19.	Self-soothe	M	T	W	TH	F	S	S
6.	Stay Focused	M	T	W	TH	F	S	S	20.	Pros and cons	M	T	W	TH	F	S	S
7.	Do What Works	M	T	W	TH	F	S	S	21.	Radical Acceptance	M	T	W	TH	F	S	S
8.	DEAR MAN	M	T	W	TH	F	S	S	22.	Opposite Action	M	T	W	TH	F	S	S
9.	GIVE	M	T	W	TH	F	S	S	23.	Positive reinforcement	M	T	W	TH	F	S	S
10.	FAST	M	T	W	TH	F	S	S	24.	Validate self	M	T	W	TH	F	S	S
11.	Cheerleading Statements	M	T	W	TH	F	S	S	25.	Validate someone else	M	T	W	TH	F	S	S
12.	Identifying & labeling emotions	M	T	W	TH	F	S	S	26.	Think/Act dialectically	M	T	W	TH	F	S	S
13.	PLEASE MASTERY	M	T	W	TH	F	S	S	27.	Building A Healthy Routine	M	T	W	TH	F	S	S
14.	Half Smile	M	T	W	TH	F	S	S	28.	Cognitive restructuring	M	T	W	TH	F	S	S

Adolescent Daily Diary Card

Name: _____   Week of: _____

Urges				Self Harm		Suicidal		School	Emotion: Anger	Emotion: Fear	Emotion: Joy	Emotion: Misery	Emotion: Pain	Emotion: Sad	Emotion: Shame	Skills *
	Drugs			Thoughts 0-5	Actions Y/N	Thoughts 0-5	Actions Y/N	Urge to Cut Class 0-5	0-5	0-5	0-5	0-5	0-5	0-5	0-5	
	Alcohol	Street Drugs	Prescription Drugs													
Mon.																
Tues.																
Wed.																
Thurs.																
Fri.																
Sat.																
Sun.																

0-5
0 = Not at all   3 = Rather Strong
1 = A bit   4 = Very Strong
2 = Somewhat   5 = Extremely Strong

*Skills
0 = Not thought about or used
1 = Thought about, not used, didn't want to
2 = Thought about, not used, wanted to
3 = Tried, but couldn't use skills
4 = Tried, could use skills, didn't help
5 = Tried, could use skills, helped
6 = Didn't try, used skills, didn't help
7 = Didn't try, used skills, helped

148

Appendix E

This is a sample or template for a Behavior Analysis Chain, sometimes called a BCA. There are many different versions and you can use ours, or make your own!

BEHAVIOR ANALYSIS

- Chain analysis for analyzing target behavior in a situation.

WHAT IS THE MAJOR TARGET BEHAVIOR THAT I AM ANALYZING?

WHAT PROMPTING EVENT IN THE ENVIRONMENT STARTED ME ON MY CHAIN TO MY TARGET BEHAVIOR?

WHAT THINGS IN MYSELF AND IN THE ENVIRONMENT MADE ME VULNERABLE?

WHAT SPECIFICALLY WERE THE CONSEQUENCES IN THE ENVIRONMENT?

Immediate   →
Delayed   →

IN MYSELF

Immediate   →
Delayed   →

BEHAVIOR ANALYSIS

WHAT ARE WAYS THAT I CAN REDUCE MY
VULNERABILITY IN THE FUTURE?

WHAT ARE WAYS THAT I CAN PREVENT THE
PROMPTING EVENT FROM OCCURRING AGAIN?

WHAT HARM DID MY TARGET BEHAVIOR CAUSE?

WHAT ARE MY PLANS TO REPAIR, CORRECT, AND/OR
OVER-CORRECT THE HARM?

MY SINCERE FEELINGS AND THOUGHTS ABOUT THIS
THAT I WANT TO SHARE:

References

[1]Linehan, M. (1993a). Cognitive-behavioral treatment of borderline personality disorder. New York: Guilford

[2] Miller, A., Rathus, J., Linehan, M. (2007). Dialectical behavior therapy with suicidal adolescents. Guilford Press, New York/ London.

[3]Linehan, M. (1993b). Skills training manual for treating borderline personality disorder. New York: Guilford

ABOUT THE AUTHORS

Kimberly Christensen, MA, LPP is currently a therapist and DBT skills trainer for children and adolescents. She earned her Master's of Arts degree in counseling psychology from the University of St. Thomas and is currently pursuing her doctorate degree in counseling psychology at the University of St. Thomas. She has completed Dr. Linehan's 10-Day Intensive Training Course in DBT and has also received training from the same institution on How to be a Skills Trainer. She resides in Minnesota with her husband and two cats. Her outside interests include hiking, canoeing and golfing.

Gage Riddoch, PsyD, LP, MSW, CDP, is a DBT skills trainer, specializing in the treatment of children and adolescents. He received his doctorate in clinical psychology from Pacific University and his masters degree in social work from Savannah State University. Gage has received DBT skills training from Behavior Tech, LLC on How to be a Skills Trainer. Gage is also a chemical dependency professional in the state of Washington. He currently resides in Heidelberg, Germany with his wife and pet skunk. His interests include animal-assisted therapy, tennis, and water sports.

Julie Eggers Huber, PsyD, LP is a clinical psychologist practicing in the Brainerd Lakes area. She has completed the Dr. Linehan's 10-Day Intensive Training Course in DBT provided by Behavioral Tech, LLC. For nearly the past decade, she has worked with adolescents struggling with a vast array of psychiatric problems, focusing on the application of DBT interventions, milieu development, and outcome evaluation. She also specializes in the application of Equine Assisted Psychotherapy. She resides in the country, enjoying mindful experiences with loons, horses, dogs, and gardening.

Made in the USA
Middletown, DE
18 February 2016